T0311809

Cambridge Elements ≡

Elements in the Philosophy of Mind
edited by
Keith Frankish
The University of Sheffield

MENTAL ILLNESS

Tim Thornton
University of Central Lancashire

CAMBRIDGE
UNIVERSITY PRESS

CAMBRIDGE
UNIVERSITY PRESS

University Printing House, Cambridge CB2 8BS, United Kingdom

One Liberty Plaza, 20th Floor, New York, NY 10006, USA

477 Williamstown Road, Port Melbourne, VIC 3207, Australia

314–321, 3rd Floor, Plot 3, Splendor Forum, Jasola District Centre,
New Delhi – 110025, India

103 Penang Road, #05–06/07, Visioncrest Commercial, Singapore 238467

Cambridge University Press is part of the University of Cambridge.

It furthers the University's mission by disseminating knowledge in the pursuit of
education, learning, and research at the highest international levels of excellence.

www.cambridge.org
Information on this title: www.cambridge.org/9781108925020
DOI: 10.1017/9781108939836

© Tim Thornton 2022

First published 2022

A catalogue record for this publication is available from the British Library.

ISBN 978-1-108-92502-0 Paperback
ISSN 2633-9080 (online)
ISSN 2633-9072 (print)

Mental Illness

Elements in the Philosophy of Mind

DOI: 10.1017/9781108939836
First published online: May 2022

Tim Thornton
University of Central Lancashire

Author for correspondence: Tim Thornton, TThornton1@uclan.ac.uk

Abstract: The very idea of mental illness is contested. Given its differences with physical illnesses, is it right to count it, and particular mental illnesses, as genuinely medical as opposed to moral matters? One debate concerns its value-ladenness, which has been used by anti-psychiatrists to argue that it does not exist. Recent attempts to define mental illness divide both on the presence of values and on their consequences. Philosophers and psychiatrists have explored the nature of the general kinds that mental illnesses might comprise, influenced by psychiatric taxonomies such as the *Diagnostic and Statistical Manual* and the *International Classification of Diseases,* and the rise of a rival biological 'meta-taxonomy': the Research Domain Criteria (RDoC). The assumption that the concept of mental illness has a culturally invariant core has also been questioned. This Element serves as a guide to these contested debates.

Keywords: mental illness, classification, transcultural psychiatry, concept of disorder, looping kinds

ISBNs: 9781108925020 (PB), 9781108939836 (OC)
ISSNs: 2633-9080 (online), 2633-9072 (print)

Contents

Introduction

This Element examines some of the controversies and debates concerning mental illness. Much more so than physical or bodily illness, the very idea of mental illness and illnesses is subject to critical scrutiny and impassioned disagreement. This occurs at the level of the generality of the question: does mental illness, as such, exist? But, also, particular illnesses are questioned. Is, for example, attention deficit hyperactivity disorder (ADHD) a real illness, or is it merely the normal distraction and disruption experienced by some children? The latter *may* be negatively valued by society and teachers without being indicators of a medical kind.

Even more contentious examples are personality disorders: disorders of deep-seated and long-term behaviour and experience, generally related to difficulties in interpersonal relations. The American Psychiatric Association's *Diagnostic and Statistical Manual-5* (*DSM-5*) subdivides personality disorders into ten kinds grouped into three clusters. The diagnostic criteria for cluster B personality disorders, including borderline personality disorder, seem to be highly value-laden, giving rise to the accusation that they are primarily moral rather than clinical conditions (Charland 2006). Such an objection need not take for granted that the moral and the medical must be distinct realms. It is enough to serve as a challenge that negative evaluations need not imply medical pathologies. The challenge for a defence of the pathological status of putative mental illnesses that do carry moral connotations is to establish that they are not merely expressive of *moral* opprobrium.

Sceptics of the diagnostic category of ADHD or personality disorders do not usually question the existence of the behavioural phenomena that underpin a psychiatric diagnosis of illness but question whether those signs really signal illness or pathology. Hence, although empirical factors are relevant to both the general and the particular debates, the debates also raise conceptual or philosophical issues of what constitutes an illness, disease, or disorder.

In the sections that follow, I will (occasionally) use the word 'madness' to indicate in a rough and ready general manner the phenomena that are typically agreed by all parties in debates about the status of mental illness or illnesses. (While some may find this word offensive, it has been adopted as a positive non-medicalised term by many mental health service user activists, and I happily use it of my own illness.) I will (more often) use 'illness' to designate a medicalised view of madness as a genuine, albeit distinct, form of pathology, suitable for medical intervention.

Some authors place weight on distinctions between illness, disease, and disorder. The American Psychiatric Association, for example, favours the term 'disorder' and offers a general definition of mental disorder (see Section 1). The philosopher Christopher Boorse proposes a value-free definition of 'disease' and then defines 'illness' as a subcategory of it meeting further constraints. The psychiatrist and philosopher Bill Fulford argues that illness, a more directly experiential notion, is logically prior and that disease is an abstraction from it. In what follows, except where setting out specific views, I will place no weight on these distinctions and generally use 'illness' to cover them all.

Given that the very idea of mental illness and illnesses is questioned, there is no easy neutral starting point. But since the focus of attention is usually the class of putative mental illnesses recognised as such by psychiatry, after highlighting some of the prima facie puzzles about mental illness and its apparent difference from physical illness, Section 1 will briefly describe the history of the two main psychiatric taxonomies – the World Health Organisation's (WHO) *International Classification of Diseases* (*ICD*) and the American Psychiatric Association's *DSM* – and set out the definition of mental disorder that was added to the third main revision of the *DSM*.

Sections 2 and 3 set out and assess general analyses of illness (or disease or disorder) offered by psychiatrists, psychologists, and philosophers. Section 2 begins with one of the key challenges they face: Thomas Szasz's argument that mental illness cannot exist because it is a contradiction in terms. A key distinction in the various accounts is whether 'illness' (or 'disease' or 'disorder') is value-free or value-laden one. Section 3 ends with an assessment of an argument presented by the philosopher Neil Pickering that the form of argument used both by Szasz and by those opposing him could never resolve the issue of whether mental illness as such or particular putative mental illnesses really are illnesses.

Section 4 examines what type of category (what kind of kinds) that putative mental illnesses might be, assuming that some, at least, exist, including a challenge raised by the National Institute of Mental Health (NIMH)'s Research Domain Criteria (RDoC) that the existing classifications may be attempting to carve nature in the wrong places.

Section 5 examines the philosopher Ian Hacking's suggestion that mental illness kinds are novel in being neither natural kinds – as many defenders of contemporary psychiatry have assumed – nor merely lying in the eye of the beholder, as critics have assumed. Instead, they might be 'looping' or 'inter-active' in that the existence of the label directly affects those who fall under it, which can cause the kind itself to mutate.

Section 6 examines the status of transcultural psychiatry, increasingly recog-nised in the *DSM*, and considers the prospects for balancing some claim to objectivity in psychiatric classification with a genuine and substantive cultural variation.

It may come as a surprise that in conclusion, I offer no general analysis of mental illness, nor a definitive view of its status. But I take it that philosophy's main aim need not be a definition or reductionist analysis but rather the exploration of the conceptual geography of puzzling notions with the aim of shedding light on them in whatever way is possible. To naturalise, that is, to place puzzling concepts less puzzlingly into a conception of nature, need not require reduction (Thornton 2019: 12–17). While still genuinely perplexing, mental illness is a useful concept and is value-laden or normative, but its values are sui generis medical values and its norms are essentially related to a notion of health, though the fundamental connections between mental health and broader notions of flourishing will not be explored in this brief Element.

1 Mental Illness and Psychiatric Diagnosis

> Madness is a subject that ought to interest philosophers; but they have had surprisingly little to say about it. What they have said, although often interesting and important, has failed to penetrate to the properly philosophical centre of the topic. They have concerned themselves with its causes and effects, with its social and ethical implications, but they have said little that is useful or definitive about what it is in itself. Preoccupied with its accidents, they have failed to engage with its essence.
>
> (Quinton 1985: 17)

Why is madness, and its conceptualisation as mental illness, philosophically interesting and worthy of scrutiny? As is common in a number of more well-established philosophical topics, one reason is that it is subject to a puzzling but everyday tension.

On the one hand, madness or mental illness is a well-known phenomenon. It is said to be experienced by a significant proportion of the world's population though accurate statistics are hard to determine. (According to data from the Institute for Health Metrics and Evaluation's Global Burden of Disease, about 13 per cent of the global population suffer from some kind of mental disorder (Charlson *et al.* 2019).) Self-reporting of the symptoms of mental illness is reasonable grounds to seek primary medical care. Diagnosis of severe illness can serve as an excuse or exculpation in law and equally can be a justification for being detained involuntarily for treatment under the Mental Health Act. It is thus subject to legal codification. Mental illness is stitched into the fabric of everyday life. Distressing and debilitating though it is, it seems to be an ordinary hardship of human existence for which medical care is, where possible, an appropriate remedy.

On the other hand, madness or mental illness sometimes seems to combine aspects of the medical and non-medical but value-laden realms. The insanity defence in law allows for acts that would otherwise be morally bad to be exculpated as expressions of illness, sometimes summarised in the question 'mad or bad?' More recently, the debate about whether feelings of bereavement should count as natural and functional experiences or as expressions of depression can be summarised as 'mad or sad?' Madness is conceptualised as illness and pathology, just as physical or bodily illness is, and yet it concerns the mental rather than the bodily. If illness is constituted as a deviation from a norm, then, at first sight at least, it looks as though mental and physical illnesses answer to different norms. That prompts the question of why the phenomena and experiences that constitute madness are conceptualised medically – as mental illness – rather than in some other way, for example, in moral or other value-laden terms.

This uneasy combination is long-standing. According to the philosopher Antony Kenny, the idea of *mental* health and illness has a specific origin in the history of ideas: Plato's *Republic*. 'The concept of mental health was Plato's invention. Metaphors drawn from sickness are no doubt as old as metaphor itself . . .. But nothing in Greek thought before Plato suggests that the notion of a healthy mind was more than a metaphor'. (Kenny 1969: 229)

Kenny argues that Plato applied the standard 'medical' humoral model of the time – according to which health depended on a balance of the elements of the constitution – to 'disorders of the soul', identifying three main constituents: reason, appetite, and temper. Although developing what appears to be a *moral* concept of mental health, Plato was, according to Kenny, intent on assimilating the moral to a *medical* model. Kenny compares Plato's approach to a similar assimilation of the moral to the medical which, he argues, was made in the 1959 Mental Health Act. This introduced to English law the concept of the psychopath: a medical diagnosis based, apparently, on a moral judgement.

Furthermore, there seems to be a number of obvious general differences between mental and physical illnesses. Champlin suggests:

1) No mental illness can be fatal, mortal, deadly or terminal in the way that some physical illnesses can be. No one can die of schizophrenia, or indeed of any mental illness at all, as you can die of smallpox or malaria . . ..
2) Mental illness is never a trivial affair of brief duration or minor importance, as are some minor childhood ailments . . ..
3) At the earliest stages of life, in the cradle and even in the womb, you may suffer from a physical illness, say, jaundice. But it makes no sense to suppose that a two-hour old baby has depression, paranoia, pyromania, kleptomania, etc . . ..

4) No mental illness can be spread by infection in the way that many physical diseases are …. These differences are *so* profound that they do seem to support the view that any connection between physical and mental illness will be paper thin, no more than nominal. (Champlin 1989: 25–6)

Champlin's characterisation is open to question. Mental illnesses do play a causal role in some deaths. Anorexia can lead to starvation, for example, even if there is always a logically sufficient more proximal explanation of the death in physical illness terms. And there can be brief episodes of mental illness. Nevertheless, Champlin's descriptions of typical differences help motivate the question of whether it is correct to classify mental and physical illnesses as species of the same genus. Perhaps the concepts of mental and illness are not so suited for each other, after all.

A second reason for philosophical interest in mental illnesses comes from the ambiguous status of apparent historical continuities. It is tempting, for example, to view the modern diagnosis of depression as continuous with long-standing notions of melancholy and melancholia and thus to think that the latter helps ground the former. But, as the philosopher of psychiatry Jennifer Radden argues, while depression and melancholy/melancholia overlap in some features, they differ in others (Radden 2009). Like depression, melancholia combined sadness with anxiety, was unreasonable and objectless, involved self-centred oversensitivity, and was associated with restless manic exaltation, but it also included what would now be called delusions and also obsessions and compulsions, which lie outside the modern diagnosis of depression. Furthermore, unlike modern depression, melancholia also carried glamorous associations of intellectual brilliance and later even genius.

A third reason derives from the opposing versions of the history of mental illness in the seventeenth and eighteenth centuries. According to the philosopher and historian Michel Foucault, the mad were separated from productive members of society, using facilities that had previously been used to segregate lepers, during the 'Great Confinement' (Foucault 1989). Later, at the end of the eighteenth century, there was a second transformation in which the mad were confined in hospitals under medical doctors. However, according to Foucault, neither transformation was a response to the underlying kind 'mental illness' coming more clearly into view. Rather, the very idea of mental illness was constructed to separate unproductive members of society from productive in the service of the rise of capitalism. I will return to this contentious idea, albeit briefly, in Section 5.

A fourth reason for philosophical interest follows from this. Opponents of psychiatry argue that madness should not be thought of in medical terms and, further, that there is a contradiction in the very idea of mental illness.. The most famous proponent of this claim is the psychiatrist Thomas Szasz, who argues, partly via the claim that mental and physical illnesses are constituted by deviation from different norms, that there could be no such thing as mental illness (Szasz 1960). If Szasz were correct, then the supposed legal and ethical consequences of mental illness would be undercut. (Szasz's arguments will be discussed further in Section 2.)

Although politically opposed, Szasz is sometimes grouped together with the 1960s and 1970s countercultural movement called 'anti-psychiatry' whose members are often said to have included the psychiatrists David Cooper and R. D. Laing, the sociologist Irving Goffman, and the historian of ideas Michel Foucault. Whether or not these and other people self-identified as members of any such movement, the label 'anti-psychiatry' does help represent an intellectual opposition to medical psychiatry that finds no parallel in, say, cardiology. (A brief sketch of Foucault's social constructionist approach to medicalising madness as the illness is discussed in Section 5.)

A fifth reason is an opposition to particular psychiatric diagnoses. Perhaps the most striking recent contested (and now former) diagnosis is homosexuality, originally classed as a sexual deviation, which was officially removed from its list of psychiatric disorders by the American Psychiatric Association by a vote of its membership in 1974. But other diagnoses and symptoms remain contested. Members of the Hearing Voices Network argue that hearing voices is not the symptom of a disorder but merely a different expression of human subjectivity, akin to homosexuality. Debate continues about ADHD, which some regard as an illicit medicalisation of normal naughtiness while others campaign for its continued status as a disorder so that sufferers can continue to access medical support. Personality disorder is perhaps the most stigmatising of diagnoses, and some say (as Kenny said of Plato's model) that it medicalises a moral category. Such disputes do not seem to be simply empirical matters but rather highlight a lack of clarity as to what is meant to be 'mental illness'.

The tension between the everyday taken-for-granted status of mental illness and the suspicion that there is something fundamentally problematic about it suggests the need for philosophical inquiry.

A Thumbnail Account of the Recent History of the Classification of Mental Illnesses

The mental illnesses that are recognised by medical professionals are codified in two classificatory systems: the WHO's *ICD* and the American Psychiatric Association's *DSM*. These have been frequently revised, and the current versions are numbered *ICD-10* and *DSM-5*. Although formally independent of one another, the two systems of classification have converged so there is now a great deal of similarity.

The broad shape of both taxonomies can be traced back to textbooks of the German psychiatrist Emil Kraepelin. Starting in 1883, Kraepelin published and revised his textbook, which, unlike previous neurological attempts to ground psychiatry in brain science, was based on psychologically influenced accounts of symptoms and the course of illness that he recorded in the case notes of patients. In the sixth edition, published in 1899, Kraepelin divided mental illnesses into thirteen broad kinds (Shorter 1997: 106–9). He also divided psychotic illnesses – illnesses without an organic cause in which the subject loses 'contact' with the world and lacks insight into their own condition – into those with an affective component and those without, as follows:

> This division of [psychotic forms of] insanity into two big groups made diagnosis quite simple. If the patients were melancholic or euphoric, cried all the time, were always tired without a cause, or displayed any of the other signs of depression or mania, [i.e., their condition had an affective component] they were classed as 'manic-depressive illness'. If they were psychotic in the absence of an affective component, they had dementia praecox. If they were manic-depressive, they would probably get better; if they had what everybody was soon abbreviating as 'd. p.', they probably wouldn't. Thus by 1899, Kraepelin had elevated the two greater nonorganic ('functional') psychoses – manic-depressive illness and schizophrenia – to the top of the pyramid, where they remain in only slightly modified form to this day as the object of endeavor of serious psychiatry. (Shorter 1997: 107)

What Kraepelin termed 'dementia praecox' is the historical forebear of schizophrenia.

In addition to the apparent overlap of specific mental illnesses with contemporary classification, Kraepelin's textbook also shaped some underlying assumptions of contemporary psychiatry. In his *History of Psychiatry,* Edward Shorter summarises this influence as follows:

> In addition to providing a new way of classifying illness, Kraepelin's structure insisted that there were a number of discrete psychiatric illnesses, or diseases, each separate from the next. Depression, schizophrenia, and so forth were different just as mumps and pneumonia were different. Finally, being 'Kraepelinian' meant that one operated within a 'medical model' rather than a 'biopsychosocial' model, as the battle lines later became drawn.
>
> (Shorter 1997: 108)

Both the *ICD* and *DSM* are neo-Kraepelinian in this broad sense.

The *ICD* is the WHO's publication. In 1948, it took over a French classification dating back to 1853 and originally called the *International List of Causes of
Death* and published an expanded version called *ICD-6*, which incorporated
non-fatal illnesses for the first time, in 1951. Most chapters of the *ICD-6*
classification, those dealing with bodily disorders, were well received and
readily adopted around the world. The psychiatric section alone proved
problematic, with most countries, indeed most psychiatric institutions, continu-
ing to operate with their own systems.

The WHO commissioned the British psychiatrist Erwin Stengel to investi-
gate why this had happened and to propose a basis for a classification that would
be more widely acceptable. It was in this connection that a conference was set
up at which Carl Hempel, a philosopher of science, was invited to speak.
Stengel chaired Hempel's session, and some of Hempel's ideas provided the
basis for his report to the WHO.

In fact, the key change Stengel proposed was based on an intervention by the
UK psychiatrist Sir Aubrey Lewis. The change was to abandon attempts at
a classification based on theories of the causes of mental disorder (because such
theories were premature) and to rely instead on what could be directly observed:
that is, symptoms. The result was *ICD-8*, which was widely adopted. The
present version, *ICD-10*, and, indirectly, *DSM-5* are both derived from *ICD-8*
and retain their focus on symptoms. This was not, however, a key moral in
Hempel's paper, which instead stresses the eventual goal of theory, rather than
observation, based classifications. But psychiatry was not thought to have
reached that stage of development.

The *DSM* is the system of the American Psychiatric Association, which
formed a task force in 1948, to create a new standardised diagnostic system. At
the time, there were five separate diagnostic classification systems being used
in the United States in different settings, including the insane asylum system,
the Army system, the Navy system, the Department of Veterans Affairs
system, and the American Prison Association system (Fischer 2012). *DSM-
I*, as it became known, was based on the Veterans Affairs system and was
divided into two main sections: disorders with established organic brain
disease and disorders without brain disease. The latter disorders were labelled
'functional'. One feature of *DSM-I*, and even more so of its first revision as
DSM-II, was the presence of causal or 'aetiological' theories. Disorders were
defined as reactions to events (and in *DSM-II* as neuroses, reflecting
a Freudian heritage).

There was a parallel change within American psychiatry, which shaped the
writing of *DSM-III*. Whilst *DSM-I* and *DSM-II* had drawn heavily on psycho-
analytic theoretical terms, the committee charged with drawing up *DSM-III*

drew on the work of a group of psychiatrists from Washington University of St Louis. Responding in part to research that had revealed significant differences in diagnostic practices between different psychiatrists, the 'St Louis Group', led by John Feighner, published descriptive criteria for psychiatric diagnosis. The *DSM-III* task force replaced reference to Freudian aetiological theory with more observational criteria.

As a result, both classification systems – *ICD* and *DSM* – are light on aetiological theory, and both stress clinical signs (what the clinician can observe) and symptoms (what the patient reports). Both are thus more clearly neo-Kraepelinian than their more aetiological earlier versions. This has had a positive effect on reliability – the agreement in diagnosis by clinicians – though the effect on validity, on the ability to 'cut nature at its joints' is disputed.

The following extract is an example of the form that a codification of diagnosis takes. These are the key criteria for a diagnosis of schizophrenia in *DSM-5*.

Schizophrenia Diagnostic Criteria 295.90 (F20.9)

A. Two (or more) of the following, each present for a significant portion of time during a 1-month period (or less if successfully treated). At least one of these must be (1), (2), or (3):

1. Delusions.
2. Hallucinations.
3. Disorganized speech (e.g., frequent derailment or incoherence).
4. Grossly disorganized or catatonic behavior.
5. Negative symptoms (i.e., diminished emotional expression or avolition).

B. For a significant portion of the time since the onset of the disturbance, level of functioning in one or more major areas, such as work, interpersonal relations, or self-care, is markedly below the level achieved prior to the onset (or when the onset is in childhood or adolescence, there is failure to achieve expected level of interpersonal, academic, or occupational functioning).

C. Continuous signs of the disturbance persist for at least 6 months. This 6-month period must include at least 1 month of symptoms (or less if successfully treated) that meet Criterion A (i.e., active-phase symptoms) and may include periods of prodromal or residual symptoms. During these prodromal or residual periods, the signs of the disturbance may be manifested by only negative symptoms or by two or more symptoms listed in Criterion A present in an attenuated form (e.g., odd beliefs, unusual perceptual experiences).

D. Schizoaffective disorder and depressive or bipolar disorder with psychotic features have been ruled out because either 1) no major depressive or manic episodes have occurred concurrently with the active-phase symptoms, or 2) if mood episodes have occurred during active-phase symptoms, they have been present for a minority of the total duration of the active and residual periods of the illness.

E. The disturbance is not attributable to the physiological effects of a substance (e.g., a drug of abuse, a medication) or another medical condition.

F. If there is a history of autism spectrum disorder or a communication disorder of childhood onset, the additional diagnosis of schizophrenia is made only if prominent delusions or hallucinations, in addition to the other required symptoms of schizophrenia, are also present for at least 1 month (or less if successfully treated).

(APA 2013: 99)

The *DSM-5* Definition of Disorder

In addition to the codification of the various mental illnesses or disorders that it recognises, the current version of the American Psychiatric Association's *DSM-5* also contains a *general* definition of mental disorder.

A mental disorder is a syndrome characterized by clinically significant disturbance in an individual's cognition, emotion regulation, or behaviour that reflects a dysfunction in the psychological, biological, or developmental processes underlying mental functioning. Mental disorders are usually associated with significant distress or disability in social, occupational, or other important activities. An expectable or culturally approved response to a common stressor or loss, such as the death of a loved one, is not a mental disorder. Socially deviant behavior (e.g. political, religious, or sexual) and conflicts that are primarily between the individual and society are not mental disorders unless the deviance or conflict results from a dysfunction in the individual, as described above. (APA 2013: 20)

This is a complex and inelegant definition combining a number of elements. A disorder is (1) a clinically significant disturbance that, additionally, (2) reflects an underlying mental dysfunction and that, additionally, (3) is *usually* associated with significant distress or disability. Two further elements are ruled out: neither expectable or culturally approved responses such as to loss nor deviant behaviours in itself are disorders.

This definition raises a number of immediate questions. What counts as 'clinically significant'? Note that any answer to this question that preserves the informativeness of the definition cannot itself rely on an understanding of disorder. So 'clinically significant' cannot be analysed as meaning *signifying mental disorder*. Second, what are the grounds for saying that a disturbance *reflects* underlying dysfunction? And is the fact that such disorders are *usually* associated with distress or disability part of a definition of disorder or an empirical claim about them?

The *DSM-5* definition varies from those offered in previous editions. But the *DSM* has not always included a definition of disorder in general in addition to the specifications of particular disorders (schizophrenia, depression, mania, etc.). It was first included in *DSM-III* in 1980. According to the philosopher of psychiatry Rachel Cooper, 'The date is crucial. During the 1970s, the APA reeled under attack from both gay activists and anti-psychiatrists. Defining 'mental disorder' came to be rhetorically useful for the APA in both these battles'. (Cooper 2015: 84)

This suggests two, albeit related, roles for a definition. One is to serve as a guide for determining whether particular states or conditions count as pathologies: disordered rather than merely different. The other is to support the very idea that there can be genuine mental pathologies at all against criticisms from anti-psychiatry that the very notion is incoherent.

In the latter role, however, the current *DSM* definition does not seem to have silenced psychiatry's critics. Consider Eric Maisel's post on the website of *Psychology Today* in the year that the current version of the *DSM* was published.

> See how easy the definers of non-existing mental disorder have it. First they define it one way, as they did in the DSM-4 .... Then, under pressure by skeptics as to the whether this definition made any sense whatsoever, they redefined non-existing mental disorders this new way in the recently released DSM-5 .... The very idea that you can radically change the definition of something without anything in the real world changing and with no new increases in knowledge or <u>understanding</u> is remarkable, remarkable until you realize that the thing being defined does not exist. It is completely easy – effortless, really – to change the definition of something that does not exist to suit your current purposes .... The question is not, 'What is the best definition of a mental disorder?' The question is not, 'Is the DSM-5 definition of a mental disorder better than the DSM-4 definition of a mental disorder?' Those are absolutely not the right questions! The first and only question is, 'Do mental disorders exist?' The phenomena certainly exist. The birds and bees exist; pain and suffering exist. But birds do not prove the existence of gods and pain does not prove the existence of mental disorders. Let us not play the game of debating the definitions of non-existent things. Let us move right on.
> (www.psychologytoday.com/blog/rethinking-psychology/201307/the-new-definition-mental-disorder)

The nature of the disagreement between this view and the views of the authors of the *DSM* is striking. The latter hold both that mental illness and particular illnesses exist. This review denies the former and hence the latter. That is not to deny that the particular phenomena that are construed in the *DSM* as indicators of illness exist. But Maisel denies that they constitute illnesses. This invites the following questions. How can such fundamental disagreement about the existence of mental pathology continue? What is the connection between the phenomena that both sides agree exist and mental illness? And can this disagreement be rationally resolved? The next two sections will consider the issue at the level of the general concept of mental illness, or disorder and madness. Sections 4 and 5 will examine the kinds of kinds that mental illnesses might be. Section 6 will discuss cultural variation in mental illnesses.

Summary

Mental illness – the medicalised view of madness – raises conceptual issues of philosophical significance for a number of reasons, including its contested history and historical continuity. It is codified in two similar works – the *DSM* and *ICD* – which are both revised periodically. Possibly in response to criticism of the very idea of mental illness by the so-called anti-psychiatry movement and also in response to controversy concerning particular putative mental illnesses, such as homosexuality (no longer so classed), ADHD, and personality disorder, the *DSM* now contains a general definition of mental disorder. But it has done little to silence critics.

2 Philosophical Analyses of Mental Illness: Szasz, Kendell, and Boorse

In the previous section, I set out some of the puzzles that the idea of mental illness raises, the recent history of the codification of mental illnesses in two international psychiatric taxonomies, and the attempt, in one of them, to suggest a general definition of mental disorder. In this section and the next, I will examine some more philosophically promising accounts of mental illness, disorder, or disease. One theme will be the contested role and significance of values.

Szasz's Null Hypothesis

One of the incentives for the development of an analysis of disorder by both psychiatrists and philosophers was a response to anti-psychiatric criticisms of psychiatric diagnosis. Although he also distanced himself from anti-psychiatry – calling it 'quackery squared' (Szasz 2009) – key arguments against the very idea of mental illness were set out by the US psychiatrist Thomas Szasz in his critique of psychiatry.

The centrepiece of Szasz's critique is an article and then a book called *The Myth of Mental Illness* (Szasz 1972). Szasz claims that the everyday assumption that mental illnesses exist just as much as physical illnesses do has two lines of support, both of which he rejects. One is based on the relation between mental illnesses and illnesses (or diseases) of the brain. The other depends on the idea of sui generis mental illnesses.

Szasz's first line of argument *against* mental illness is based on criticising an argument in defence of it by its relation to illnesses of the body or brain. It is drawn from the idea that, for example, 'syphilis of the brain' or 'delirious conditions' produce disorders of thinking and behaviour. A hypothetical argument in *defence* of mental illness can now run as follows. If all mental illnesses are illnesses of the brain and if illnesses of the brain are real, then mental illnesses are real. Szasz offers two criticisms of this argument. The first is that there is a distinction between the ability of neurological defects to explain bodily symptoms – such as a defect of vision – and their supposed ability to explain abnormal thought. 'Explanations of this sort of occurrence . . . must be sought along different lines' (Szasz 1972: 13).

The second criticism is also based on drawing a distinction in this case between physical symptoms such as fever or pain (sic) and mental symptoms. The latter, unlike the former, turn crucially on aspects of the relation between sufferer and clinician. If a person reports that he or she is Napoleon, this only counts as a mental symptom if he or she is *not* Napoleon. This, in turn, Szasz suggests, involves a 'covert comparison between the patient's ideas . . . and those of the observer and the society in which they live' (ibid: 14). It is worth noting that Szasz's argument goes a little too quickly in that it blurs the distinction between how we might *know* that a subject is deluded – perhaps by comparison with what we think – and what it *is* to be deluded. That is, he blurs epistemology and ontology here. But the underlying point is that assessment of mental symptoms is normative in a way that assessment of physical symptoms is not. 'The notion of mental symptom is therefore inextricably tied to the *social*, and particularly the *ethical*, *context* in which it is made, just as the notion of bodily symptom is tied to an *anatomical* . . . context' (ibid: 14).

Taken together, these two criticisms are designed to head off the idea that mental illness can be defended by its relation to bodily illness.

> For those who regard mental symptoms as signs of brain disease, the concept of mental illness is unnecessary and misleading. If they mean that people so labelled suffer from diseases of the brain, it would seem better, for the sake of clarity, to say that and not something else. (ibid: 14)

What then of the idea that mental illness is sui generis: a form of illness like physical or bodily illness but essentially and distinctly mental? Szasz offers two arguments that I will here refer to as the swift argument and the longer argument. In fact, the swift argument can be interpreted in two ways.

Szasz suggests that the root of the claim that mental illness is sui generis is the idea that mental illness is a 'deformity of the personality' that explains human disharmony or more generally life problems. His response to this idea is swift:

> Clearly, this is faulty reasoning, for it makes the abstraction 'mental illness' into a cause of, even though this abstraction was originally created to serve only as a shorthand expression for, certain types of human behaviour. (ibid: 15)

This dense argument can be unpacked a little. Since the seminal analysis of causation provided by the Scottish philosopher David Hume, it has been widely held that causal connections are contingent connections: they do not hold of necessity. Contingency is an essential feature of causation. Thus, if the connection between a putative cause and its effect is not contingent but necessary, then it cannot be genuinely causal. Szasz's argument can then be restated. If mental illness is defined in terms of certain sorts of behaviour, then the connection between it and those forms of behaviour is necessary, not contingent. Thus, it cannot cause that behaviour. But that is what it was supposed to do. Thus, there is no such thing. (For an argument that Szasz's view presupposes a discardable assumption of behaviourism, see Kelly *et al.* 2010.)

The second, related but longer, argument that Szasz deploys against a sui generis conception of mental illness runs as follows.

> The concept of illness, whether bodily or mental, implies deviation from some clearly defined norm. In the case of physical illness, the norm is the structural and functional integrity of the human body. Thus, although the desirability of physical health, as such, is an ethical value, what health is can be stated in anatomical and physiological terms. What is the norm, deviation from which is regarded as mental illness? This question cannot be easily answered. But whatever this norm may be, we can be certain of only one thing: namely, that it must be stated in terms of psychological, ethical, and legal concepts . . . . [W]hen one speaks of mental illness, the norm from which deviation is measured is a *psychosocial and ethical* standard. Yet the remedy is sought in terms of *medical* measures that – it is hoped and assumed – are free from wide differences of ethical value. The definition of the disorder and the terms in which its remedy are sought are therefore at serious odds with one another . . . . (ibid: 15)

> Since medical interventions are designed to remedy only medical problems, it is logically absurd to expect that they will help solve problems whose very existence have been defined and established on non-medical grounds. (ibid: 17)

Thus, there are two separate and incompatible sets of norms, deviation from which supposedly constitutes illness. On the one hand, there are structural and functional norms for physical or bodily illness. On the other hand, there are psychological, psychosocial, ethical, and legal norms for supposed mental illnesses. The problem, according to Szasz, is that subscribers to the idea of mental illness also insist that it can be addressed using medical measures. But these are designed for, or perhaps characterised by reference to, the structural and functional norms of bodily illness. That is why it is 'logically absurd' to expect them to be appropriate. It is a kind of 'category error' (in the phrase of the philosopher Gilbert Ryle (Ryle 1949)).

Szasz thus offers a kind of null hypothesis for the concept of mental pathology or disorder. There could be no such conditions. That is not to say that he denies that there is mental suffering. He does not deny the existence of the phenomena that are taken to constitute mental illness in this sense. These are 'problems of living'.

> While I maintain that mental illnesses do not exist, I obviously do not imply or mean that the social and psychological occurrences to which the label is attached also do not exist. Like the personal and social troubles that people had in the Middle Ages, contemporary human problems are real enough. It is the labels we give them that concern me, and, having labelled them, what we do about them. (ibid: 21)

This helps characterise the position of those who deny that the *DSM-5* definition picks out anything in the world. They do not need to deny human suffering or problems of living. They dispute that these should be thought of as mental illness or disorder paralleling the realm of physical illness or disorder.

Szasz himself suggests that the application of the notion of illness to the mind is a metaphor that has become 'literalised', that is:

> treating a metaphorical disease as a disease instead of as a metaphor. This is an absurd mistake few of us would make if the word used metaphorically was not as weighty as the word *disease* ... Clearly saying that the drink is a *metaphoric screwdriver* is not saying that it is some other kind of screwdriver; it is saying that it is *not a screwdriver at all*. (Szasz 1987: 150)

I will briefly return to the idea that mental illness is a metaphorical notion in the conclusions at the very end of this work.

The rest of this section and the following one will examine attempts to block Szasz's argument by proposing conceptions of disorder that permit mental as well as physical disorders. (For an attempt to block Szasz's argument, even granted his view of the relevant norms, see Thornton 2007.)

Kendell's and Boorse's Naturalistic and Value-Free Accounts

Two influential defences of the idea of mental illness were offered in 1975 by Christopher Boorse and Robert Kendell. Like Szasz, Kendell was a professor of psychiatry, but unlike Szasz, he was an establishment figure. In a paper called 'The concept of disease and its implications for psychiatry', he argues in defence of mental illnesses or diseases by suggesting a method for assessing the status of mental illness based on a definition of illness in general: []'Before we can begin to decide whether mental illnesses are legitimately so called we have first to agree on an adequate definition of illness; to decide if you like what is the defining characteristic or the hallmark of disease'. (Kendell 1975: 306)

Reviewing the history of the debate, he comments as follows: 'By 1960 the 'lesion' concept of disease, and its associated assumptions of a single cause and a qualitative difference between sickness and health had been discredited beyond redemption, but nothing had yet been put in its place. It was clear, though, that its successor would have to be based on a statistical model'. (ibid: 309)

But, as Kendell goes on to say, whilst a statistical model, based on the idea that illness is an unusual condition, may address some of the weaknesses of a single-lesion model, statistical abnormality by itself cannot distinguish between 'deviations from the norm which are harmful, like hypertension, those which are neutral, like great height, and those which are positively beneficial, like superior intelligence' (ibid: 309). Some further criterion is needed to address the fact that illness is a specific kind of deviation from the norm.

Kendell's preferred solution, in this paper, is based on the work of the British chest physician J. G. Scadding.

> Scadding was the first to recognise the need for a criterion distinguishing between disease and other deviations from the norm that were not matters for medical concern, and suggested that the crucial issue was whether or not the abnormality placed the individual at a 'biological disadvantage' ... He defines illness not by its antecedents – the aetiological agent or the lesion producing the overt manifestations – but by its consequences. In itself this is not new; previous attempts to define illness as a condition producing suffering or as meriting medical intervention had done the same but ... [had] proved inadequate. The concept of 'biological disadvantage' differs from these, however, in being more fundamental .... (ibid: 309)

Scadding does not define 'biological disadvantage', but Kendell argues that it must involve increased mortality and reduced fertility, 'whether it should embrace other impairments as well is less obvious' (ibid: 310). Thus, he uses this criterion to test the idea of mental illness.

> Do mental illnesses possess the essential attributes of illness or not? Do they, by reducing either fertility or life expectancy, produce a significant biological disadvantage? (ibid: 311)

After some investigation – which turns on empirical facts about the effects of these putative illnesses – he is able to come to a modest, positive conclusion.

> Schizophrenia, manic depressive illness, and also some sexual disorders and some forms of drug dependence, carry with them an intrinsic biological disadvantage, and on these grounds are justifiably regarded as illness; but it is not clear whether the same is true of neurotic illness and the ill-defined territory of personality disorder. (ibid: 315)

The following three things are worth noting about Kendell's approach:

1. He does not attempt to show that mental illnesses are illnesses because they are also, really, physical illnesses. He thus avoids one line of criticism expressed by Szasz.
2. His criterion of illness is general. It applies to physical and mental illness. Any condition is an illness if it leads to biological disadvantage of the right sort. That said, it is originally derived from considerations of paradigmatic physical illnesses.
3. The criterion is purely factual and value-free. It is a matter simply of empirical fact whether a condition increases mortality and reduces fertility. If it does, then it is an illness. If not, then not. (Since the condition is a conjunction, strictly if merely one conjunct is satisfied that is not sufficient to count. Of course, it might plausibly be interpreted as a disjunction: increased mortality *or* reduced fertility.)

Kendell's approach faces a dilemma, however. On the one hand, he inherits from Scadding ambiguity about what 'biological disadvantage' means. Without some further explanation, it will not shed light on the nature of the mental illness. But, on the other, attempting to solve that problem by appeal to the idea of increased mortality and reduced fertility produces a substantial theory of illness or disease but one which is vulnerable to the objection that it does not articulate what is *essential*. Roughly speaking, it seems plausible that one might be genuinely ill without this leading to increased mortality and reduced fertility. Whilst those measures might well address illnesses that, specifically, are life-threatening and undermine reproductive ability, neither risk seems to be an essential feature of *everything* that we might call 'illness' or 'disease'.

The US philosopher Christopher Boorse also attempts to articulate a value-free, purely descriptive account of disease but using a conceptually richer notion: that of biological function in general. He argues that our understanding of mental health should be informed by root notions of health in general, drawn from physical medicine. This in turn leads him to frame a definition of health and illness, or rather disease, in general in what he hopes will be value-free terms. Boorse, unlike Kendell, distinguishes between the concepts of disease and illness. Disease is supposed to be the more fundamental notion and value-free. Illness is a disease that is 'serious enough to be incapacitating' and 'undesirable for its bearer' (Boorse 1975: 61). Hence, it is only disease for which Boorse offers a value-free definition.

> An organism is healthy at any moment in proportion as it is not diseased; and a disease is a type of internal state of the organism which:
>
> i) interferes with the performance of some natural function – i.e. some species-typical contribution to survival and reproduction – characteristic of the organism's age
> ii) is not simply in the nature of the species, i.e. is either atypical of the species, or, if typical, mainly due to environmental causes.
>
> (Boorse 1976: 62)

This analysis introduces a key extra concept compared with Kendell's model. Natural functions are prima facie *normative*. That is, they imply a notion of correct functioning. Whether they can account for the *failure* of function is a little more complex, as I will explain. At the same time, modern advocates of natural functions claim that they are purely descriptive and scientific terms. The idea of a biological function – something being *for* something – does not imply the irreducible idea of values, for example, those of a designer.

There are two rival dominant philosophical accounts of functions, one associated with Robert Cummins and another with Larry Wright. Cummins argues that the function of a biological subsystem is whatever it normally *currently does* that contributes towards the goals of a larger system (Cummins 1975). Wright, by contrast, argues that the function of a biological subsystem is fixed by its natural selective history, what the subsystem *was selected to do* (Wright 1973). One potential advantage of the latter is that it may more easily support a notion of failure of function: a mismatch between the historical function and present dispositions. By contrast, on the Cummins view, if a functional explanation does not apply, there is no function rather than a dysfunction or failure of function.

Boorse supports a Cummins-style view that a function pertains to functional explanations of current system performance. But not any fortuitous contribution to survival and reproduction counts as the function of an organism's subsystems. A function is a 'statistically typical contribution to individual survival and reproduction' (Boorse 1997: 8). Thus, although functions have a normative dimension beyond brute cause and effect, this is still analysed using statistical notions. Similarly, disease is not just an impairment of normal function but additionally one which is 'either atypical of the species, or, if typical, mainly due to environmental causes' (ibid: 8). It is this addition of statistical norms to functional explanation that promises to solve the problem of dysfunction just mentioned. Hence, Boorse aims to balance the apparent normativity of health and illness – the idea that health is an organism functioning correctly and disease is a dysfunction – with a conception of nature that excludes values. Like Kendell, Boorse's account is 'naturalistic'.

This, however, presents a problem (see especially Kingma 2007). The statistically typical contribution to individual survival and reproduction that various biological subsystems of humans make varies according to age and sex. But changes in such contributions – for example, the effects of the ageing of muscles – can be perfectly normal aspects of average health. And hence, specifying an atypical failure of function – to pick out disease – requires an appropriate reference class. For the muscular weakness of an eighty-year-old man to be atypical requires comparison with a population of appropriate age and not, for example, teenagers. But there is an unlimited number of ways of articulating possible references classes. So what principle underpins the selection of relevant reference classes?

This difficulty can be highlighted with an example. Suppose that the failure of well-regulated cell division in one person is compared with a reference class of cancer sufferers whose cell division is similarly unregulated. Against such a group, the former individual's failure of function – failure to contribute to survival and reproduction – will not be atypical. And hence, it will not count as diseased. But by what principle is the class of cancer sufferers excluded as a relevant reference class? The problem is that the obvious answer – that reference classes should be relevant to *healthy* subpopulations – begs the very question of the difference between health and illness that Boorse's account is supposed to answer.

Summary

In response to the challenge that Szasz raises to the very idea of mental illness, based on the idea that mental and physical illness answer to distinct norms, both Kendell and Boorse offer general analyses of the concept of illness that are supposed to account for mental illness too. While Szasz assumes that putative mental and physical illnesses are deviations from different norms, with the former value-laden and the latter not, Kendell and Boorse dispute this and offer value-free accounts of mental illness. Both accounts face difficulties, however.

In the next section, I will two examine accounts that accept that mental illness is value-laden but dispute Szasz's sceptical conclusions. I will also examine a philosophical argument that the form of argument explored in both these sections could not rationally resolve the argument as to whether madness or mental illness really is – or can be – genuinely a matter of medical pathology.

3 Philosophical Analyses of Mental Illness: Wakefield, Fulford, and Pickering

In the previous section, I introduced Thomas Szasz's challenge to mental illness and two attempts at responses to it. Both Kendell and Boorse attempt to counter Szasz's argument that mental illness is value-laden, while physical illness is not by offering a value-free conception of both physical and mental illness. In this section, I will examine Jerome Wakefield's and Bill Fulford's very different value-laden accounts. At the end of the section, I will outline Neil Pickering's attempt to stand back from and shed light on all these accounts (and others) and to argue that the form of argument they all share – Szasz and his critics – cannot rationally settle the status of putative mental illness.

Wakefield's Harmful Dysfunction Account

Jerome Wakefield – a professor of social work – proposes an account of disorder that supplements the value-free or naturalistic idea of dysfunction with the value-laden notion of 'harm'. Disorders, whether mental or physical, are harmful dysfunctions. Like Boorse, the idea of dysfunction or failure of function is supposed to be value-free because it is based on a naturalistic analysis of function. Wakefield differs from Boorse, however, by adopting the other dominant philosophical approach to natural functions: that for which a subsystem was historically selected.

Roughly speaking, on this view, the function that a particular trait of an organism exemplifies explains the past evolutionary success and survival value of that trait. The biological function of a trait and its behaviour can diverge. This point is sometimes put by saying that what matters is not which traits or dispositions are selected but what *function* they are selected *for*. This distinction can be illustrated by the example of a child's toy (Sober 1984). A box allows objects of different shapes to be posted into it through differently shaped slots in the lid. The round slot thus allows the insertion of balls, for example. It may be that the actual balls allowed through or 'selected' in one case are all green. But they are selected *for* their round cross section and not their green colour. Ruth Garrett Millikan stresses the fact that the biological function of a trait may be displayed in only a minority of actual cases. It is the function of sperm to fertilise an egg, but the great majority of sperm fails in this regard (Millikan 1984: 34).

Since biological functions can diverge from mere dispositions (the box does not have the function of selecting green balls, even though it tends to do that), they have the extra resources necessary for accounting for the *failure* of function. The distinction between success and failure of a system, organism, or organ can be defined by reference to its functioning in accord with its naturally selected biological function.

Wakefield's work on mental illness is in this tradition. He relies on an account of natural function drawn from evolutionary theory to distinguish those dispositions that accord with a system's naturally selected function from those that do not.

> A natural function of a biological mechanism is an effect of the mechanism that explains the existence, maintenance or nature of the mechanism via the same essential process (whatever it is) by which prototypical nonaccidental beneficial effects ... explain the mechanisms which cause them ....
>
> It turns out that the process that explains the prototypical non-accidental benefits is natural selection acting to increase inclusive fitness of the organism. (Wakefield 1999: 471–2)

As the previously given example of sperm suggests, however, failures of function may be widespread in cases that would not intuitively be described as disorders. And hence, Wakefield argues that while dysfunction is a necessary element of disorder, it is not sufficient. The addition of the qualification 'harmful' provides an appropriate practical clinical focus on the relevant subset of all dysfunctions that call for treatment.

Although the analysis contains the value term 'harm', the core notion of dysfunction is supposed to be value-free and naturalistic. This has, however, been criticised by both the psychiatrist and philosopher Bill Fulford and the Aristotelian philosopher Christopher Megone. In a lengthy commentary called 'Nine variations and a coda on the theme of an evolutionary definition of dysfunction', Bill Fulford attempts to eliminate all terms that are either apparently value-based or 'genuinely' teleological (purposive) from Wakefield's definition of failure of function (Fulford 1999). His aim is to show that this task fails and thus that Wakefield fails to reduce the concept of function to austere descriptive terms. Thus, the main weight of Fulford's argument occurs as he discusses the final 'variation', or possible interpretation, of Wakefield. Here, he makes two suggestions. One is that:

> [I]f organisms, as distinct from rocks and winds, have purposes, then, in addition to the causal language of evolution, we can (non-metaphorically) speak of them teleologically . . .. The nonmetaphorical use of teleological as well as causal language of organisms is not as such anti-scientific . . .. All the same the necessity for teleological ... language in this context directly conflicts with Wakefield's express aim of establishing a purely causal theory. And this aim ... in turn reflects the fact that teleological language – purposes, intentions, motives, means and ends – is, from the point of view of a conventional picture of science, uncomfortably close to values.
>
> (Fulford 1999: 416)

Without some further argument, however, this is not decisive. Wakefield is following the tradition of attempting to 'naturalise' purposive talk by showing how it is really purely causal talk in disguise. He does this through the idea that natural selection can underpin a definition of function that is not evaluative. If this were successful, it would enable him to talk of biological functions or biological purposes, and thus failures of function, secure in the knowledge that this was merely a shorthand for an austere description of underlying causal processes. This is not to say that Wakefield is successful in this reduction, but something more is needed to indicate that this appeal to natural selection fails.

Megone provides a different argument against Wakefield's descriptive account of function as follows:

> According to Wakefield, on this model, "the heart exists for the purpose of pumping the blood in the sense that past hearts having this effect causally explains how hearts came to exist and be maintained in the species and the genesis of the heart's detailed structure". (Wakefield 2000: 31)
>
> The most basic difficulty here is that past hearts' pumping the blood figure in all sorts of causal stories, stories in which agents die young, or agents do not reproduce, or agents reproduce but defectively, and so on. It is not the case that hearts pumping the blood have simply caused hearts to exist. So hearts pumping the blood does not causally explain how hearts came to exist. This cannot therefore be the sense in which the pumping of the blood is a functionally explicable activity of the heart. (Megone 2000: 60–1)

Whilst there is something right about this objection, to which I will return shortly, it is noticeable that Megone runs together causal *explanation* and mere causal *relations*. By contrast, Wakefield relies on specifying the function of systems through what best *explains* their evolutionary fitness. Thus, he can reply that the divergent causal *relations* do not *explain* the heart's existence. Recall again the distinction between the dispositions of a system and its natural function. Its dispositions are genuine causal consequences of the system's nature but do not explain its existence.

Nevertheless, Wakefield's account faces a number of challenges. Dominic Murphy and Robert Woolfolk list a number of possible objections that stem from the central idea that biological dysfunction is *necessary* for disorder (Murphy and Woolfolk 2000). One objection is that disorders may arise from failings in social learning. If fed the wrong information, even functioning mental modules may generate deviant behaviour. And even where evolution plays a role, there are challenges. Murphy and Woolfolk raise the case of mental spandrels. 'Spandrel' is a term used by Gould and Lewontin, who suggest that what appear to be adaptations may actually be by-products of adaptive traits, just as spandrels in church architecture are the result of the design of load-bearing arches (Gould and Lewontin 1979). Mental spandrels would be mechanisms that are the by-product of evolution but without designed functions themselves. Murphy and Woolfolk suggest that they might nevertheless produce apparently pathological behaviour. A similar possibility is that some mental subsystems are vestigial mechanisms – the mental equivalent of the appendix – which would lack functions and hence could not fail to function according to Wakefield's analysis. A third possibility is that some apparent pathologies – as defined by the *DSM* – might be produced by mechanisms performing their naturally selected function. Murphy and Woolfolk suggest that antisocial personality disorder and histrionic personality disorder may be functioning traits selected for 'acquiring group resources without adhering to norms governing the acquisition of social status' (Murphy and Woolfolk 2000: 244). 'Free-riding' on a social group without reciprocation may be a biological successful strategy despite its cost in social harmony and unpopularity. Wakefield's response to such criticism is generally to bite on the bullet and insist on the connection between disorder and dysfunction. In cases where there is a lack of biological dysfunction, there really is no disorder. He thus argues, for example, that both depression and anxiety disorders are overly inclusive diagnoses (Horwitz and Wakefield 2007).

A more serious objection concerns pathologies of the behaviour of traits that were selected not for those behaviours (Bolton 2008; Kingma 2013; Lilienfeld and Marino 1995). Dyslexia, for example, is, prima facie, a pathology. But, because humans developed writing comparatively recently and in only some locations, the ability to read cannot explain the selective advantage of whatever widespread trait underpins it. Hence, the ability to read is not the biological function of that trait. And hence dyslexia cannot be a dysfunction of that trait. Wakefield's response is to argue that the ability to read must be the effect at a remove of a trait selected for some other function. Hence, there is a dysfunction somewhere. But as both Bolton and Kingma argue, that is a contingent empirical claim. It does not follow from the fact that there is a prima facie pathology in the effects at a distance of a trait with a selected-for function that there is a dysfunction in that trait. If this were even a testable hypothesis case by case, it would be up to subsequent science to discover which diagnostic categories really are disorders as Wakefield theorises. It would be an open question how many psychiatric diagnostic categories are 'disorders' in this sense.

Murphy and Woolfolk also consider the objection that we presently lack sufficient knowledge of evolutionary history to determine functions. They report that:

> Wakefield's response to this criticism is the claim that we can recognize a malfunctioning mental mechanism if we have 'sufficient indirect evidence – e.g., surface evidence that indicates or correlates with the existence of internal dysfunction – to infer that some mechanism is failing to perform as designed' (1997b: 255). According to Wakefield, if we have someone who exhibits behavior that is disproportionate to environmental stressors, we can infer that an evolved mechanism has malfunctioned (1997a).
>
> (Murphy and Woolfolk 2000: 246)

But as they stress, this seems to reverse the priority of evolutionary theory and clinical judgement in determining mental function and dysfunction.

> How are we to decide what is a 'normal' or 'proportionate' response to environmental stress? Are such decisions entirely objective, as Wakefield contends, or are they underlaid by value judgments? To proceed as Wakefield suggests, we have to decide how 'dysfunction-indicating' a behavior is in whatever context it occurs; e.g., whether there has been a 'real loss' prior to the depressive symptoms. We often must rely on 'the clinician's common sense understanding of normality' (Wakefield 1992: 244) in order to discriminate proportionate (nondysfunctional) responses from disproportionate responses. (ibid: 246)

This is what seems right about Megone's criticism. The kind of evolutionary 'just-so' story that is supposed to underpin genuine dysfunctions, and hence, disorders itself relies on clinical judgements about what a well-functioning mind is.

Fulford's Value-Laden Failure of Ordinary Doing Account

So far, in this and the previous section, I have set out Szasz's claim that mental illness is a value-laden concept and hence incoherent, Kendell's and Boorse's claim that it is value-free, and Wakefield's analysis that factors mental illness into a value-free core notion of dysfunction and the additional value of harm. In the final two parts of this section, I will outline two, more general, attempts to offer insight into the underlying disagreements in the debate.

The first is provided by Bill Fulford. Taking Szasz, Kendell, and Boorse to represent the debate, Fulford argues that all agree that mental illness is conceptually difficult, and by contrast, physical illness is straightforward in part because the latter is value-free. From this, they deduce value-free criteria for illness and apply them to mental illness with different results. As described previously, Szasz argues that supposed mental illnesses are deviations from value-laden norms and thus do not meet the value-free criteria for illness. Kendell argues that they do fit his preferred criteria of increased mortality and decreased fertility. Boorse argues that they fit his account based on a biostatistical analysis combining biological functions and statistical norms.

Fulford argues, however, that the assumption that Szasz, Kendell, and Boorse share is wrong. Physical illness is not value-free. It merely seems that way because we tend to agree on the values that underpin physical health and illness, whilst there is much more variation in the values governing mental health and illness. Furthermore, it is a general feature of value judgements that when we agree on underlying values, they can become disguised by value-free criteria.

He argues that the same contrast applies to mental and physical illness. It is because mental healthcare is concerned with areas of human experience and behaviour, such as emotion, desire, volition, and belief, where people's values are highly diverse, that it seems more value-laden than physical illness. This contrast between divergent values in mental healthcare and shared values in physical medicine explains why there is an anti-psychiatry but not an anti-cardiology movement.

In suggesting that illness is a value-laden concept, Fulford is not attempting to reduce it to some other, better-understood values. Medical values are distinct from moral and aesthetic values, for example (Fulford 1989: xiii). But he does suggest that they are connected to the values involved in the action. Fulford's positive account of the nature of illness draws on the idea of 'ordinary doing' as the kind of action that one 'gets on and does' without having to try, without having intentions explicitly in mind (Austin 1957). A failure to be able to do this kind of thing, in the absence of external constraint, captures, he suggests, the character of experiences of illness. Furthermore, it is an essentially value-laden notion because it inherits the values involved in reasons for action. Illness is a failure to do the kind of thing one wants to do and is ordinarily able to do. This highlights the negative value that seems to attach to illness.

Like Boorse, and unlike Kendell and Wakefield, Fulford suggests that illness and disease are distinct. But unlike Boorse – who offers a value-free account of disease and then derives a further value-laden account of illness – Fulford thinks that illness is the root notion and that diseases are conditions that cause illnesses and hence inherit their connection to values.

It is harder to criticise Fulford's account than the others because his aim is not to reduce illness to more basic concepts but to show the connections – the logical geography – between it as a concept and others. One objection Fulford attempts to anticipate is that chronic pain, for example, is not itself a failure of ordinary doing but nevertheless seems to be pathological. He suggests that it is still a component in the 'machinery of action' in that it is something one would normally do something *about* (ibid: 133–8). Withdrawing one's hand from a flame is a typical piece of ordinary doing. So having a pain from which one is unable to withdraw *involves* a failure of ordinary doing in the relevant sense of illness even if the pain itself is not the failure of doing. This suggests that Fulford's account is disjunctive: illness is one thing or another, though related. But it highlights the way in which he is not offering a reductionist account of illness but rather suggesting characteristics of the sorts of conditions we call illness.

This suggests that there is a question that such an account will not be able to address. If illness is an internally generated failure of ordinary doing, what of weakness of will or failures generated by moral failure or failure of character or resoluteness? If this were a reduction of the concept of illness to the concept of action, for example, it would owe an account of which 'internal' factors constituted illness and which not. But I think that it is a mistake to see the account in this way. The relevant forms of internal failure are those which involve the medical values involved in illness. The account *displays* conceptual connections rather than analysing illness in non-illness-presupposing terms. Fulford's account could not be used to defend mental illness, from neutral first principles, against those who question its illness status because it presupposes sui generis medical values. This connects to the reason why the *DSM* definition of disorder seems unable to silence the objections of anti-psychiatry mentioned at the start of the previous section. I will now turn to a diagnosis of why that might be the case.

Pickering and the Likeness Argument

I suggested earlier that the *DSM-5* definition of disorder has not silenced anti-psychiatric criticism. In this part, I will set out one reason why this may be so. In his book *The Metaphor of Mental Illness* (Pickering 2006), the philosopher Neil

Pickering suggests that attempts to defend the illness status of mental illness as a whole or particular conditions such as schizophrenia are unsuccessful because of shared dependence on what he calls the 'likeness argument', which he argues, is fundamentally flawed.

According to Pickering, the likeness argument is supposed to resolve the status of mental illness by showing that putative mental illness is, indeed, sufficiently like illness. It does this in one of two ways. Either, it takes a paradigmatic form of illness, a specific case like hypertension or physical illness more generally, and shows that mental illness is sufficiently like it because it shares sufficient of its features. Or, it abstracts a generic concept of illness (again, typically from physical illness) and shows that mental illness fits sufficient features of that general concept to count as illness.

Why then does the likeness argument fail to settle the matter? Pickering argues that it depends on two assumptions, both of which can be questioned. He says:

> If the likeness argument is to resolve this dispute two things must, I think, be taken to be the case:
>
> 1. that there are features of human conditions such as schizophrenia, which decide what category, or kind, these conditions are a member of, and
> 2. that, with respect to the presence or absence of these features, a condition such as schizophrenia is describable independent of the category it is assigned to.
>
> (ibid: 17)

The first is a general condition derived from a view of how concepts apply to things. The suggestion is that concepts apply deductively and algorithmically in virtue of things having objective features. This stands in contrast, for example, to a view where all such concept application depends on an additional element of creativity or imagination akin to the application of a novel metaphor. The second is a more specific assumption relevant to the debate about mental illness. It is that the ascription of features to conditions – putative illnesses – can be made independently of a top-down decision as to the illness status of those conditions.

Pickering suggests that both assumptions can be questioned. Criticism of the first –the 'weak objection' to the likeness argument – typically depends on pressing the role of human interests and values in the formation of human concepts. Nevertheless, as he goes on to concede temporarily at least, there need be no incompatibility between acknowledging a role for interests and values in setting up a scheme of concepts and its autonomous application.

The 'strong objection' turns on questioning the second assumption. Pickering argues that the ascription of features to conditions – putative illnesses – depends on the overall category – illness or not – into which they are placed. The argument for this is piecemeal. In each of three cases – alcoholism, ADHD, and schizophrenia – he offers competing descriptions of their basic features manifesting first an assumption that they are illnesses and second that they are not. The behavioural features of alcoholism, for example, can equally be described in terms of moral weakness or of pathologically caused behaviour: opposing top-down theories. Pickering concludes that in contested cases, the features themselves cannot be used to determine to which overall category the condition belongs. (He goes on to note that this claim also undermines the first assumption, and thus, his earlier concession was merely temporary.)

Pickering argues that Fulford's analysis shows a partial insight into this but that Fulford fails to appreciate that the lessons apply to his own account too.

> Though Szasz and Kendell both recruit a paradigm likeness argument, Fulford notices that each calls upon different features [Szasz highlights 'deviation from the clearly defined norms of the structural and functional integrity of the body'; Kendell highlights 'biological disadvantage'] of his chosen paradigm (physical illness) in order to prove his case. This explains, as Fulford neatly points out, why despite the fact that both use the likeness argument, they manage to reach opposite conclusions. As a result, neither can necessarily hope to convince the other, or anyone else for that matter, and the radical question goes unresolved. This clearly presents a problem in using the paradigm version of the likeness argument, which is one of Fulford's principal points. However, it turns out that Fulford is not objecting to the likeness argument as such, for he too uses it ... abstracting ... a generic concept of illness (action failure) from paradigmatic physical examples of illness, and employing that to try and resolve the question of whether mental illness exists, by showing that action failure defines illness, and is a principal feature of conditions such as schizophrenia and alcoholism. (ibid: 16)

Applied to the question raised at the end of the previous discussion of Fulford, this reflects the difficulty in assessing whether a condition should count as an 'internally generated failure of ordinary doing' understood medically – and hence count as illness for Fulford – or instead count as a failure of resolution or moral weakness and hence be a moral 'problem of living'. That is, even if Fulford's model of disorder – or any other – were accepted as correct, it might still not settle which conditions were and which were not genuine mental illnesses.

Pickering's criticism focuses on the form of the likeness argument, and he argues that there is a principled reason why it cannot rationally settle fundamental disputes about mental illness. His central claim is that detectable and observable features of a condition, a putative illness, cannot be described without begging the question of the pathological status of that condition. This is not, however, a surprising claim. If the correct description of the features is taken to imply a pathological status then, trivially, it cannot be independent of that overall status. This is an essential feature of an argument to the effect that something is an illness in virtue of sharing the features of illnesses. If the features of illnesses are agreed, then anyone who wishes to dispute whether a particular condition is an illness – for example, ADHD – then they must dispute whether ADHD shares those features.

Furthermore, it is hard to see what could be wrong with the likeness argument itself, given its triviality. (If the possession of a particular kind of characteristic implies illness status and if a condition has a characteristic of that kind, then it is an illness.) But, in the context of debates about mental illness, there is a further factor present. As a matter of fact, there often seem to be rival descriptions of phenomena available that differ from each other by being on opposite sides of a distinction between the medical and the moral, 'the mad and the bad'. In the final section of this work, I will return to Pickering's own account of the status of mental illness.

Summary

Over the last two sections and starting with the current official definition of mental disorder in *DSM-5*, I have outlined a number of rival accounts of the nature of the disorder and the challenges they face. The challenges depend in part on whether the accounts propose value-free naturalistic or value-laden normative accounts. The former face the additional problem of accounting for the prima facie normativity of illness: that it is a condition in which something is, in some sense, *wrong*. The latter have to address the question of whether the value is a single non-medical value (Wakefield) or a sui generis medical value or values (Fulford), and if the latter, what kind of insight into the nature of disorder the account offers. No account of disorder is without problems.

I have also suggested that there is reason to think that agreeing on an analysis of disorder may not help address the key question of whether mental illnesses or disorders really exist or whether the conditions so described are better construed in other, non-medical terms, as anti-psychiatry has long maintained.

Before returning to this in the concluding section of this Element, the next two sections will look at categories, types, or kinds one level down: not the nature of mental illness as such but the nature of mental *illnesses*. (Section 6 will look at cultural variation in mental illness.) Can the kinds set out in the *DSM* and *ICD* classifications be construed as natural kinds?

4 Vindicating Kinds

The discussion in the previous sections has concerned the analysis of the general concept of mental illness or disorder. A key question is whether the general concept of mental illness is value-laden or not. As I described in Section 1, the diagnoses of specific mental illnesses are codified in two main classificatory systems: the *DSM* and *ICD* (APA 2013; World Health Organization 1992). These catalogue illnesses and criteria for their diagnoses. And hence, alongside the debate about the nature of mental illness in general, there has been related debate about the status of this sort of classification. Reflecting the debate about the status of mental illness in general, the main philosophical focus has been the nature and status of the kinds set out in the catalogues and their natural, or other, status. This section will introduce the debate about whether mental illness classifications are natural kinds.

Different Kinds of CategoriesKinds of Mental Illness

Both the *DSM* and *ICD* taxonomies have undergone periodic revision, and there has been a long-standing debate about the form they should take. For example, should mental illnesses be thought of as categories distinct from normal health or as a continuous variation from it (akin to blood pressure or IQ)? During the period of revision leading to the publication of *DSM-5* in 2013, the psychologist Peter Zachar and the psychiatrist Kenneth Kendler published what they called a 'conceptual taxonomy' for psychiatric disorders (Zachar and Kendler 2007). In it, they set out six 'critical dimensions' or debates concerning the nature of psychiatric taxonomy. These include the following:

1) causalism versus descriptivism,
2) essentialism versus nominalism,
3) objectivism versus evaluativism,
4) internalism versus externalism,
5) entities versus agents, and
6) categories versus continua. (ibid: 557)

If it were possible to settle these debates in advance, then that would help determine the proper form of a classification of mental illnesses, which could help shape the revision of the *DSM*. The difficulty of this project is, however, illustrated even in Zachar and Kendler's own paper. I will demonstrate this using two of their examples: objectivism versus evaluativism and internalism versus externalism, then draw some general conclusions, and finally examine two rival approaches to thinking about psychiatric kinds.

The first distinction, between objectivism versus evaluativism, is defined as follows:

> Is deciding whether or not something is a psychiatric disorder a simple factual matter ('something is broken and needs to be fixed') (objectivism), or does it inevitably involve a value-laden judgement (evaluativism)? (ibid: 558)

The example suggested here for objectivism is surprising. It does not seem to be a *simple* factual matter, a matter to be contrasted with an evaluation, whether something is *broken and needs to be fixed*. Contrast this idea with a paradigmatic objective taxonomy such as the periodic table in chemistry. The periodic table classifies on the basis of atomic number (the number of protons in the atomic nucleus). To model this example on that would require thinking of 'needing to be fixed' as an objective property of the layout of the world, which is there anyway, like atomic number, irrespective of the values of a judging subject. It would be a property the detection of which would be enough, without complementary desires, to motivate a subject to bring about its repair. Against a stark contrast of facts and values, such an objective and yet at the same time essentially motivating property would seem, using John Mackie's term, 'queer' (Mackie 1977: 38–42). Evaluativists, by contrast, might indeed claim that values make up part of the fabric of the world and are essentially motivating properties (see Thornton 2002). But they belong to the other side of the distinction from the one which Zachar and Kendler are attempting to illustrate.

In fact, even the first element of the example is not such a simple descriptive idea. Being broken is not a simple physical property. Nor need it even supervene on (simple) physical properties since, for example, a device that is broken with respect to one function might successfully possess a different function.

These considerations suggest that inverting the role of the example in the definition would be better:

> Is deciding whether or not something is a psychiatric disorder a simple factual matter (*objectivism*), or does it inevitably involve a value-laden judgement (*evaluativism*) ('something is broken and needs to be fixed')?

Two things, however, could help rationalise the choice of example. First, outside the explicit contrast with a value judgement, there is something obviously right in saying that whether something is broken and needs to be fixed is treated as a factual matter that can be of a simple and everyday kind. Unprejudiced by a sharp distinction of fact and value, one would naturally say that this is the kind of thing that can be the content of a judgement. A small child viewing a damaged bicycle wheel might take in both that it is broken and the corresponding need for it to be repaired at a glance.

Second, whilst it may not have the conceptual simplicity of atomic number, the example more closely reflects the kind of taxonomic kinds found in psychiatry. Objectivists – as contrasted with evaluativists – will have to be able to analyse such claims – broken and needs to be fixed – in value-free and objective terms. The task is fundamentally harder for objectivists than for evaluativists as the former are committed to a purely factual analysis, whereas the latter allow both facts and values; evaluativists are not committed to a values-only analysis of disorder. In picking this example, Zachar and Kendler are, whether deliberately or by accident, implicitly drawing attention to the challenge for objectivists. The choice of example, however, suggests a Fulfordian moral (from Section 3): it is easy to ignore the evaluative element in a judgement when there is widespread agreement as to the values.

Zachar and Kendler's distinction between internalism versus externalism is summarised as follows:

> Should psychiatric disorders be defined solely by processes that occur inside the body (*internalism*), or can events outside the skin also play an important (or exclusive) defining role (*externalism*)? (ibid: 558)

They further characterise the distinction with the following hints. Modern psychiatry has been largely internalist and holds that events within the body are 'critical for understanding and defining' mental disorders (ibid: 558). Externalists are either moderate and hold that 'what goes on inside the head cannot be isolated from an organism's interaction with the world', or radical, in taking external events to be definitional, as exemplified in syndromes that are considered to be 'reactions to harsh societal demands' (ibid: 559).

It is helpful to draw attention to a further distinction that Zachar and Kendler do *not* make but that can shed light on their distinction. One can think of externalism as characterising a claim about either causation or constitution. If one thinks, plausibly, that environmental factors sometimes cause mental illness, then one is a causal externalist. But one may think that they cause mental illness by affecting states – perhaps neurological – *within* the body. Such a position is causally externalist but constitutively internalist. An example from physical medicine is the idea that poverty can cause – in the sense of raising the probability of – heart disease. Given that poverty is abstract, it might seem that a biomedical cardiologist could not possibly accept such a claim. But they can via the idea that poverty can cause poor diet and that poor diet can lead to high cholesterol, arterial deposits, and hence heart dysfunction. Such a sketch of the causal mechanism combines a social cause and an internalist model of the constitution of illness. (Constitution is not quite the same thing as what *defines* a mental illness. Even a constitutional internalist may find it helpful to label illnesses by their broader causes. Post Traumatic Stress Disorder labels an illness by a historical cause but could be assumed to be an internal dysfunction of the brain, nonetheless.)

This clarification can be applied to an example of externalism that Zachar and Kendler give, the interpersonal model:

> Contrary to any of the medical models, an interpersonal systems model is staunchly externalistic. Most fundamentally, this model views disturbed behaviour as arising from disturbed relationships. Rather than deriving from psychopathology in individuals, psychiatric disorders are seen to develop dynamically from pathology in interpersonal contexts. The notion of patients being containers of internal psychological states is minimised, whereas the view of them as persons trying to adapt to their social worlds is maximised. The context or the interpersonal system is both locus of pathology and the cause of pathological behaviour. (ibid: 562)

Most of the characterisation in this passage would fit a causally externalist but constitutively internalist view of the disorder. The fact that disturbed behaviour *arises* from disturbed relationships is consistent with the causation being mediated by states of the brain. Similarly, dynamic changes in response to interpersonal contexts may be dynamic changes of the brain. And there is no reason to rule out a central role for brain-mediated responses for persons *adapting to* social worlds. The 'context as cause', in the final sentence of the previous passage, again exemplifies merely *causal* externalism.

The difficulties that Zachar and Kendler's discussion faces suggest the difficulty of attempting to ground a view of psychiatric kinds from first principles. Rational disagreement is possible even about the supposedly neutral terms of the debate as they set it out. Despite that, taking these two dimensions together suggests what is perhaps a standard view of the status of psychiatric kinds. It combines a value-laden aspect with an internalist view of the constitution. A helpful way to illustrate this was suggested independently by both Rachel Cooper and Dominic Murphy (Cooper 2007; Murphy 2006). Both suggest the analogy of mental illness kinds with weeds.

> Weeds are unwanted plants, and so whether a particular plant is considered a weed or a flower can vary with the tastes of the gardener. The umbrella category 'weed' is defined in terms of values and is not a natural kind. However the different species of weed, such as dandelion and dock, are still natural kinds. Although whether a particular plant counts as a weed

depends on values, the fact that it is a dandelion, or a dock, depends solely on its natural properties. Similarly, while the category 'mental disorder' is value-laden and does not form a natural kind, conditions that are commonly disorders – schizophrenia, depression, and so on – may still be natural kinds.

(Cooper 2013: 955)

According to the analogy, a value-laden analysis of mental disorder is consistent with the idea that once a condition is identified as an instance of that broader kind, its own identity conditions can be value-free. Although the identification of dandelions as a weed is a value judgement, the identification of a particular plant as a dandelion may be value-free. That, however, is merely to sketch a conceptual possibility. Further work is needed to offer an analysis of the nature of the categories or kinds specific sorts of mental illnesses might be. But it is enough to raise the question: is there a plausible view of kinds that would fit mental illnesses and would still count as natural or objective?

Mental Illnesses as Mechanistic Property Clusters (MPCs)

One difficulty that has affected this task has been the comparison (explicit or implicit) of psychiatry with the chemistry taxonomy, realised in the periodic table. Such an approach to taxonomy has been taken to support a form of essentialism, contrasted with nominalism in Zachar and Kendler's conceptual taxonomy (Zachar and Kendler 2007). Kendler, Zachar, and Carl Craver summarise essentialism as follows:

A standard example of an essentialist kind is an element from the periodic table. The putative essence of an element is its atomic number, the number of protons in its nucleus. Take gold. Most important properties of gold (its melting point, malleability, color, and resistance to oxidation) follow lawfully from its atomic number. Furthermore, 'real ' gold can be identified by checking if that essence is present. Every atom of gold has 79 protons. No atom that is not gold has 79 protons. (Kendler *et al.* 2011: 1144)

Essentialism connects taxonomic kinds to essences. For chemical elements, the obvious candidate for essence is their atomic number. Zachar and Kendler characterise the opposition to nominalism in their own way as follows:

A *radical nominalist* argues that we must pick our categories for their use, with no expectation that they will reflect deeper truths about the world. A *moderate nominalist*, by contrast, agrees that there is some structure of psychiatric illness in the world but there is no one unique categorization that stands above the others on *a priori* grounds.

(Zachar and Kendler 2007: 558)

To explain this contrast between essentialism and nominalism will require a short digression.

On a long-standing and influential view, from David Hume to the Logical Positivists, three apparently independent ways of dividing up truths align. These distinctions are as follows:

- Epistemological: a priori versus a posteriori (how can the truth be known? Must it be based on experience (a posteriori), or can it be known independently of experience (a priori)?)
- Semantic: analytic versus synthetic (does the truth depend only on the meaning of the words involved (analytic)? Or does it also depend on the nature of the world (synthetic)?)
- Metaphysical: necessary versus contingent (might the truth have been false (contingent), or would it remain true no matter what (necessary)?)

On the long-standing view, despite the apparent independence of these distinctions, they align. If something can be known a priori, then it is analytic (true in virtue of meaning alone) and necessary (true in all possible worlds). If it requires experience to be known, then it is synthetic and contingent. Not everyone in the history of philosophy agreed with this. Immanuel Kant, for example, argued that the truths of arithmetic were a priori and necessary but still synthetic. But it was a default mainstream view into the twentieth century.

This was challenged independently by both Hilary Putnam and Saul Kripke (Kripke 1972; Putnam 1975). They argued that the identity of natural kind terms with their underlying chemical composition was an a posteriori, synthetic, but necessary truth. If water is H_2O, it could not have been otherwise. Of course, the word 'water' could have been used to pick out something else had the history of English been different. But, used as it is, the stuff that is water had to have that chemical structure. Had the colourless liquid flowing freely on Earth been different, it would not have been water (even though it may have been called 'water').

This view is *essentialism*. The essence of water is its chemical structure. Additionally, that structure explains the various properties of water. Such a view appears to be a good fit with the kind of kinds found in chemistry's periodic table. But it does not seem to fit the diagnostic categories of the *DSM* and *ICD*, where there does not seem to be a plausible candidate for the role played by atomic structure in chemistry.

As critics often point out, despite the optimism for a change of paradigm with *DSM-5* towards a more biological approach, not a single biological criterion – or 'biomarker' – was included. No other candidate for an essence has been identified.

If essentialism were necessary to mark out a kind as a natural or objective kind, then psychiatric diagnostic kinds could not be natural. In the next section, I will consider another option as a contrast with natural kinds: Ian Hacking's 'looping kinds'. But essentialism is not the only account of natural kinds. A weaker account of natural kinds is now, perhaps, the most influential philosophical model of diagnostic kinds: Kendler *et al*'s mechanistic property cluster (MPC) model (Kendler *et al*. 2011). While, on a more traditional view, nominalism is a radical view according to which categories or kinds are names without *any* corresponding reality, the MPC model counts as a nominalist view in accord with the criteria Zachar and Kendler set out (see previous discussion and Zachar and Kendler 2007: 558).

The MPC structure is weaker in two respects than a view of psychiatry based on essences. It proposes that kinds in psychiatry are not essentialist kinds. There is neither a single property that marks them out, and they do not hold of necessity. Rather, certain properties pitched at a variety of levels – from the biological up to the social – appear together because they are stable together.

> The 'kind-ness' of species is not, from an MPC perspective, produced by a defining essence but rather from more or less stable patterns of complex interaction between behavior, environment and physiology that have arisen through development, evolution and interaction with an environment. It is this often complex and intertwined mechanism that produces the imperfectly shared characteristics of the members of a (biological) species. Such kinds are more heterogeneous than elements in a periodic table. Unlike all atoms of gold, individual members of a species need not share all their properties. Across the range of a species, some systematic differences may arise in subpopulations in coloration, body weight or food preference. Hybrids can also occur. However, the fuzziness of these boundaries does not detract from their stability. (Kendler *et al*. 2011: 1147)

A mental illness kind is thus realised at a variety of levels, and contingent laws hold them together. It is a rather looser picture than essentialism, inspired by the kinds of generality that apply to biological species.

In one of the papers cited as a source of this model, Richard Boyd points out a key difference between it and something that looks superficially similar (Boyd 1991). Ludwig Wittgenstein famously suggested that some concepts are like a family resemblance (Wittgenstein 2009: §67). Everyone in a family may look related, but this may be because some members share the family nose appearance, others the ears, others the eyes, and so forth. There are no necessary or essential features, and what makes up a sufficient likeness varies across family members. Kinds that group objects together in this manner are called 'family resemblance' kinds. Generally, philosophers have assumed that – unlike the example that gives this kind of kind its name – the connection between the features that make up such a kind is established by social convention. In another of Wittgenstein's examples, 'game' is a family resemblance concept. Particular instances count as games because they have enough features of games, but the clusters of relevant features that amount to games is a matter of social convention.

The MPC account of kinds is different because the features or properties that make up a kind are given by nature, not convention. The properties or features that enable the recognition of a biological species are by the biological laws and mechanisms that link them together in a stable way.

The MPC model looks to be a plausible fit with *DSM* categories. It is at least possible that disease categories could be species-like kinds with overlapping surface features and underlying causes permitting some variation. If so, given that the features are connected by laws rather than conventions, they would earn the right to be regarded as *natural* kinds.

This brief outline is enough to address a common critical question asked about mental illness. On the assumption that it often carries the risk of stigma, what is the point of making diagnoses? What is the advantage of categorising people and their experiences using illness kinds? The answer is that it carries explanatory and predictive value. The connection between kinds and some shared mechanisms and laws suggests the way in which inductive generalisations can be reliable in the same way that generalisations about biological species can hold good even while permitting exceptions (cf. Cooper 2013).

But the MPC model was not designed to help with some of the key questions about what makes something a pathology in the first place. One way to make that point is that it is possible that sexual orientation is also an MPC kind: with behavioural and emotional aspects and – for all we know – neurological causes. But being some sort of real kind sheds no light on pathology status or not. This is not a criticism of the MPC model but a reminder that establishing that something is a genuine induction-supporting kind is not the same as establishing that it is a kind of illness.

I wrote previously that it is 'at least possible that disease categories could be species-like kinds'. But there is no guarantee that this is the case. Assuming that prima facie illness categories are given by a kind of folk-psychological description of symptoms further refined by descriptive psychiatry, Dominic Murphy suggests that the MPC model of kinds suggests a way in which psychiatric kinds could be subsequently scientifically vindicated.

> We might take the folk concept as picking out what I have called a causal
> signature – the same distinctive pattern showing through the diversity and
> leading us to an underlying causal mechanism. In this program, folk thought
> sets the agenda for a scientific project. Science discovers the natural phenom-
> enon at which the folk concept aims ... I'll call this the *vindication project*.
> (Murphy 2014: 119)

But although this might happen, Murphy himself is sceptical.

> [T]he vindication project rests on the wager that folk attributions of mental
> disorder track genuine causal signatures, rather than just imposing a unity
> dictated by how other people strike us. This implies optimism about the
> scientific credentials of folk psychology that may not turn out to be the way
> to bet. It may be that many psychiatric diagnoses have inherited from folk
> thought a belief that certain kinds of deviance can be grouped together on the
> basis of a shared underlying process that is not in fact there. This does not
> mean that there are no natural kinds in psychiatry. There may well be genuine
> causal signatures and genuine causal mechanisms. But it may not be folk
> psychology that detects them. (ibid: 121)

One way that the wager may fail is that the weed analogy may not hold. The
class of weeds as a whole is value-laden and so is the assignment, to that
general kind, of species such as dandelions. But the identification of
a particular plant as an instance of the kind 'dandelion' – and hence as an
instance of the wider kind 'weed' – is, arguably, a matter of genetics rather
than values. But it is merely an assumption of the hypothesis that mental
illness kinds might be MPC kinds that there are stable – and, according to the
analogy, value-free – underlying kinds unifying instances. The contrary
possibility is that every instance of the diagnosis of ADHD, for example,
corresponds to a judgement of childhood naughtiness but that there is
nothing deeper than that value judgement unifying them. It might be that
the unity in the value-laden judgement of naughtiness is all that gathers
together cases of ADHD and contrasts them with the rest of the population.
Their other mental and physiological properties might be quite dissimilar.
The technical term for a relation where a higher-level kind can be imple-
mented in different structures of lower-level properties is 'multiple realisation'. ADHD might be multiply realised. If so it cannot be a single MPC.

Even if the move from an essentialist model of natural kinds to a more
permissive MPC model reduces the weight of metaphysics involved in
thinking that such kinds really cut nature at its joints, it is nevertheless
merely an assumption that the right place to look for kinds relevant to
psychiatry is the list of *DSM* or *ICD* categories. What other options are
there?

RDoC and the Proper Identification of Psychiatric Kinds

One such other option is the American NIMH's RDoC project, launched before the publication of *DSM-5*. In 2010, the director of NIMH, Thomas Insel, and colleagues set out the assumptions of RDoC.

> RDoC classification rests on three assumptions. First, the RDoC framework conceptualizes mental illnesses as brain disorders. In contrast to neurological disorders with identifiable lesions, mental disorders can be addressed as disorders of brain circuits. Second, RDoC classification assumes that the dysfunction in neural circuits can be identified with the tools of clinical neuroscience, including electrophysiology, functional neuroimaging, and new methods for quantifying connections in vivo. Third, the RDoC framework assumes that data from genetics and clinical neuroscience will yield biosignatures that will augment clinical symptoms and signs for clinical management.
>
> (Insel *et al*. 2010: 749)

In 2013, Insel published a blog post that highlighted the independence of RDoC from the *DSM* classification in a list of the former's four assumptions.

- A diagnostic approach based on the biology as well as the symptoms must not be constrained by the current *DSM* categories,
- Mental disorders are biological disorders involving brain circuits that implicate specific domains of cognition, emotion, or behavior,
- Each level of analysis needs to be understood across a dimension of function,
- Mapping the cognitive, circuit, and genetic aspects of mental disorders will yield new and better targets for treatment.

    It became immediately clear that we cannot design a system based on biomarkers or cognitive performance because we lack the data. In this sense, RDoC is a framework for collecting the data needed for a new nosology. But it is critical to realize that we cannot succeed if we use *DSM* categories as the 'gold standard'. The diagnostic system has to be based on the emerging research data, not on the current symptom-based categories. (Insel 2013)

RDoC is not a rival classificatory system to the *DSM* or *ICD* but rather a higher-level approach. Jeffrey Poland, Professor of Science and Technology Studies, argues that:

> [I]t calls for proposals that are focused on studying genetics and neural circuitry in specific research domains (e.g., functional domains such as executive function, memory, and fear) without necessarily employing DSM categories. The ultimate aim is to build a research base that will underwrite a new classification system based on genetics and neural circuitry and that will promote new approaches to treatment (especially, but not exclusively, drugs, surgery, and stimulation technologies). (Poland 2014: 53)

It is a conceptual framework that carves up domains of mental functioning and subdivides each by the variety of different levels or 'units of analysis' at which they can be studied. The philosopher Kathryn Tabb argues that

> These domains, borrowed from contemporary cognitive neuroscience, contribute one axis to the matrix that the NIMH has proposed to organize psychiatric research, and are divided into more specific 'constructs', such as 'attention', 'perception', 'working memory', and 'cognitive (effortful) control', which are all constructs under the domain 'cognitive systems'. The other axis is 'units of analysis', ranging from 'genes' to 'behavior'. By encouraging the funding of research that investigates certain dimension(s) of functioning at certain unit(s) of analysis, the RDoC changes the targets of validation from DSM disorders to any sort of phenomenon that may be viewed either as an extreme on a spectrum of human variation or as a dysfunctional structure or process. Research targets are not classes of mental disorder but rather cells on the RDoC matrix that identify a certain domain of functioning studied at a certain level of analysis.
>
> (Tabb 2015: 1052)

Insel's claim that 'mental disorders are biological disorders involving brain circuits that implicate specific domains of cognition, emotion, or behavior' is consistent with the way that RDoC has been widely taken to be promoting a biological view of mental functioning and hence, by association, of psychiatry and mental illness. A key idea is that mental functions depend on intact neural circuits. Josef Parnas accused RDoC of being both neurocentric and reductionist (Parnas 2014). But, as Rachel Tabb and Luc Faucher and Simon Goyer point out, the logic of RDoC is not intrinsically reductionist (Faucher and Goyer 2015; Tabb 2015). Rather, in principle at least, it supports a multilevel approach to explanation much as Engel's biopsychosocial model does, which also suggests that there are different levels at which relevant phenomena can be viewed (Engel 1977).

Just such a picture of different metaphysical levels was described by Oppenheim and Putnam in their classic 1958 paper 'Unity of science as working hypothesis'.

> It is not absurd to suppose that psychological laws may eventually be explained in terms of the behaviour of individual neurons in the brain; that the behaviour of individual cells – including neurons – may eventually be explained in terms of their biochemical constitution; and that the behaviour of molecules – including the macromolecules that make up living cells – may eventually be explained in terms of atomic physics. If this is achieved, then psychological laws will have, *in principle*, been reduced to laws of atomic physics . . .. (Oppenheim and Putnam 1991: 407)

Oppenheim and Putnam go on to argue that the unity of science is served by 'microreductions'. These are reductions in which:

> The objects in the universe of discourse of [the reduced science or theory] are wholes which possess a decomposition into proper parts all of which belong to the universe of discourse of [the reducing science or theory]. (ibid: 407)

They then go on to explore the consequences of this view by examining the preconditions for successfully attaining unity via microreduction. Since micro-reduction is construed as the only serious possibility for the unity of science, and since its success rests on a number of other things being the case, the goal of unification has a number of presuppositions:

1. There must be several levels.
2. The number of levels must be finite.
3. There must be a unique lowest level . . ..
4. Any thing of any level except the lowest must possess a decomposition into things belonging to the next lowest level . . ..

(ibid: 409)

On Oppenheim and Putnam's picture, things higher up are made up of, or comprise, or are constituted by, things lower down. If this view were an essential part of RDoC, it would imply that the different levels were different views of fundamentally the same phenomena, and this in turn might suggest privileging the lowest level, in accord with reductionism.

Such a view of levels presents problems for accounting how there could be causal relations between them because causation is generally thought to link independent relata whereas, on the Oppenheim and Putnam picture, things at a higher level just *are* lower-level things grouped together. (This problem has been much discussed in the philosophy of mind (e.g., Kim 1993).) It is also tempting to assume that explanatory relations should hold only *within* rather than across levels.

Partly inspired by psychiatric research – where it seems that both causation and explanation can cross levels – the neat picture of nature as comprising distinct levels has come to be criticised (e.g., Campbell 2009; Craver 2007; Murphy 2008). But such criticism does not undermine the general intuitive picture that there might be different levels at which phenomena relevant to mental functioning can be investigated as presupposed by both RDoC and the biopsychosocial model. If that is the case, then, while the *use* that is typically made of RDoC's framework might tend to focus on investigation pitched at the level of neural circuitry, the framework itself does not rule out a focus at the level of the whole person and their environment.

> RDoC has never claimed that lower level explanations should be preferred; the RDoC explicitly states that environment is a critical element in the research it fosters (though, one might wonder why this dimension is not represented on its matrix). Therefore, in theory, RDoC does not obliterate the role of the environment. Indeed, one of RDoC's preoccupations is to develop 'a more mechanistic understanding of how such factors as life events and the social environment interact with development to produce a range of observed outcomes'. (Cuthbert 2014: 30)

> In these cases, researchers are trying to develop a better-integrated multilevel theory or model of a disorder or of the development of a disorder by including the environment factors in the explanation.
>
> (Faucher and Goyer 2015: 214–15)

Despite that, however, one thing that threatens to be lost as one moves from a higher level to a lower level is the very idea of *pathology*. The lower down one goes, the more the descriptions are of what happens, of what causes what. But pathology requires a notion of good and bad functioning. So one question is whether RDoC changes the subject away from human distress and illness to how brains work. The *DSM* level categories look closer to human distress and illness because they are explicitly supposed to be groupings of kinds of pathology.

Jerome Wakefield, who himself subscribes to the harmful dysfunction model of mental illness (see Section 3), presses this point.

> The DSM/ICD identifies conditions that, judging from surface symptoms, context, and background knowledge of normal human functioning, fall under the concept of disorder .... Whatever its errors, DSM/ICD remains an attempt to delineate the domain of psychological conditions that fall under the concept of disorder. RDoC offers nothing to replace the DSM/ICD efforts to delineate the domain of disorders and provide a target at which construct validation can aim. DSM/ICD provides the only thoughtful guidance to what conditions the RDoC must explain in terms of malfunctioning circuits. (Wakefield 2014: 38)

Underlying this criticism is the idea that the very idea of malfunctioning circuits – by contrast with, for example, merely differently functioning ones – requires a higher-level description. Wakefield holds that this must be couched in terms of biological dysfunction and evolutionary theory. But a parallel point holds for other accounts of the concept of mental illness in general.

This suggests that whatever insight research carried out under the RDoC framework offers into human mental functioning and its biological underpinnings, the task of charting mental illness and illnesses has to retain a connection to a level where the idea of pathology makes sense (see Thornton 2020). If arguments to exclude the prima facie evaluative nature of illness fail – as the account in Section 3 suggested – then this, in turn, highlights the central role of person-level descriptions where such values have their logical home.

Summary

There is an ongoing debate about the kinds of kinds that make up the main categories of mental illness diagnostic categories. But despite the fact that they do not look like the paradigmatic and possibly essentialist kinds in some sciences, there is no general reason to think that mental illnesses could not be a weaker form of a natural kind such as an MPC. It may be, however, that psychiatric kinds can be located at the level of symptoms and neural circuitry rather than illness syndromes. But such finer-grained and lower levels look less likely to shed light on the distinction between mental health and illness.

5 Hacking on Looping or Interactive Kinds

In the previous section, I examined perhaps the most influential philosophical model of psychiatric kinds: the mechanical property cluster model of psychiatrist Ken Kendler, psychologist Peter Zachar, and philosopher Carl Craver, developed from Richard Boyd's homeostatic property cluster model (Boyd 1991; Kendler *et al.* 2011). I highlighted the way in which it seems to be a plausible fit to the kind of kinds found in the *DSM* and *ICD*. Less strict than many models of natural kinds, it would still explain how such kinds could support the sort of inductive inferences, supporting diagnosis and prognosis, to which psychiatry aspires. I contrasted it with a rival approach – NIMH's RDoC project – that rejects the diagnostic groupings found in the *DSM* in favour of finer-grained and multilevel research foci, concentrating especially on neural circuits and their biology.

It appears to be an open empirical question as to whether RDoC might underpin a form of classification that undermines the authority of the present *DSM* and *ICD* descriptive approaches. However, RDoC does not, in itself, seem able to demarcate the boundary between mental health and illness and hence to address the key question of Sections 2–3. While RDoC may aspire to identify natural kinds of some sort at a level finer than *DSM* and *ICD* classifications, it does not address the naturalness or otherwise of the distinction between illness and other forms of difference such as moral standing.

This section will consider a contrasting account of kinds that has been developed to fit psychiatry by the philosopher of science Ian Hacking: looping or interactive kinds. These promise to provide a contrasting view of psychiatric taxonomy. To assess the very idea of looping or interactive kinds, I will first provide an overview of the context in which Hacking introduces them, then look to what 'looping' might comprise. I will suggest some scepticism about whether Hacking's account really offers a novel view of mental illnesses.

Looping or Interactive Kinds and Social Constructionism

Hacking starts his paper 'Making up people' with the following question, drawing on the work of the philosopher and historian of science Arnold Davidson:

> Were there any perverts before the latter part of the nineteenth century? According to Arnold Davidson, 'The answer is NO ... Perversion was not a disease that lurked about in nature, waiting for a psychiatrist with especially acute powers of observation to discover it hiding everywhere. It was a disease created by a new (functional) understanding of disease'. Davidson is not denying that there have been odd people at all times. He is asserting that perversion, as a disease, and the pervert, as a diseased person, were created in the late nineteenth century. Davidson's claim, one of many now in circulation, illustrates what I call making up people. (Hacking 1991: 161)

He goes on to connect both Davidson's work and his own to that of the philosopher and historian Michel Foucault: 'there is a currently more fashionable source of the idea of making up people, namely, Michel Foucault, to whom both Davidson and I are indebted' (ibid: 164).

Foucault's account of the history of mental illness and hence its constitution *as* mental illness turns on two key sociopolitical shifts. In the seventeenth century, there occurred a 'Great Confinement' in which the mad, alongside beggars, criminals, layabouts, and prostitutes, were separated from productive members of society using facilities that had previously been used to segregate lepers. Whereas the mad had previously been tolerated as eccentrics within society and even displayed in royal courts, they were now removed from the view of productive society.

> The necessity, discovered in the eighteenth century, to provide a special regime for the insane, and the great crisis of confinement that shortly preceded the Revolution, are linked to the experience of madness available in the universal necessity of labor. Men did not wait until the seventeenth century to 'shut up' the mad, but it was in this period that they began to 'confine' or 'intern' them, along with an entire population with whom their kinship was recognized. Until the Renaissance, the sensibility to madness was linked to the presence of imaginary transcendences. In the classical age, for the first

time, madness was perceived through a condemnation of idleness and in a social immanence guaranteed by the community of labor. This community acquired an ethical power of segregation, which permitted it to eject, as into another world, all forms of social uselessness. It was in this other world, encircled by the sacred powers of labor, that madness would assume the status we now attribute to it. (Foucault 1989: 54)

Later, according to Foucault, there was a second transformation, at the end of the eighteenth century, in which the mad were now confined in hospitals under the supervision of medical doctors. But Foucault's claim is that these changes were not *responses* to the nature of mental illness but that the idea of mental illness, by contrast with a broader notion of madness and social eccentricity, was *constructed* in response to broader social and economic forces.

[T]he constitution of madness as a mental illness, at the end of the eighteenth century, affords the evidence of a broken dialogue, posits the separation as already effected, and thrusts into oblivion all those stammered, imperfect words without fixed syntax in which the exchange between madness and reason was made. The language of psychiatry, which is a monologue of reason about madness, has been established only on the basis of such a silence. (Foucault 1989: xii)

The historian Andrew Scull offers a similar story (Scull 1989). According to him, an intellectual battle in the nineteenth century between a moral view of mental illness and a medical view was decided in favour of the latter by social and political factors. Crucially, the growth of capitalism required a distinction be drawn between those who genuinely could not work in factories but deserved support and those, perhaps malingers, who merely chose not to work. A medicalised view of mental illness and its management fitted the bill.

On this family of approaches, the very notion of mental illness was invented as a way to help structure society in support of the rise of capitalism. This – contested – historical account offers reason to think that the apparently real and worldly property of 'having a mental illness' is not after all such an objective matter. Rather, it is, in part at least, a projection onto the world of the needs of (capitalist) society. We call people 'mentally ill' so as to impose social and political structures on them, not because we are responding to a real division between mental health and illness in nature. Of course, there must be *some* behavioural and experiential differences that serve as the prompting for the projection, but in some sense to be determined, they do not naturally comprise illness features. Calling them an 'illness' – on the understanding of illness as a medical condition – is *not just* responding to prior biological or medical facts.

The underlying historical account has been contested. Edward Shorter summarises it, and his robust rejection of it, as follows:

> Dominating the field for the past two decades have been scholars who doubt the very existence of psychiatric illness, believing it to be socially constructed. These writers have attempted to trivialize the illnesses of the inmates and to make the case that capitalist society was venging itself on the patients for their unwillingness to work, for a Bohemian lifestyle, or even for a revolt against male authority. Thus society's growing intolerance of deviance is said to have led to the confinement of ever greater numbers of 'intolerable' individuals. It is astonishing that this interpretation could have achieved such currency as there is virtually no evidence on its behalf.
>
> (Shorter 1997: 54)

I will take no view on this historical debate. It will also be helpful to contextualise Hacking's looping kinds to offer an exaggeratedly sharp distinction between what I will call 'debunking' and 'non-debunking' social-historical accounts of natural science, such as the codification of madness as mental illness (for the use of 'debunking', see Latour 2005: 100). I will do this using an example from the recent history of physics, discussed in the social history of science (Collins and Pinch 1998): cold nuclear fusion in a test tube. This non-medical example illuminates debunking approaches because it turns on explanations of apparently objective and non-social phenomena in sociological or human-centric terms. Since mental illness is centrally a feature of human experience, of human subjectivity, it is easier to explain the distinction with a simpler and apparently objective example.

In 1989, Martin Fleischmann and Stanley Pons, chemists at the University of Utah, announced that they had achieved nuclear fusion, the process that powers the sun, at room temperature by passing an electric current through a beaker of heavy water, in which deuterium had replaced hydrogen (Collins and Pinch 1998: 57–77). They claimed that they had detected excess heat and nuclear by-products. Shortly afterwards, Steven Jones of Brigham Young University announced, independently, that he had detected fusion also using an electrolytic cell. Other laboratories immediately attempted to reproduce the supposed process, universally concluding that they could not, and a period of controversy followed. It is generally accepted that the initial results were mistaken and that cold nuclear fusion is impossible. Why?

Collins and Pinch give a detailed account of the evidence deployed and counterclaims made in the debate and thus explain how the closure was reached. As sociologists of science, they follow the following maxim:

> We try to put our readers into the shoes of the scientists, sharing [with the reader] only the knowledge that the scientists could have had at the time.
>
> (ibid: 166)

In fact, even this is not straightforward as, as their own account of cold fusion reveals, scientists often act on what they think they know, but according to later consensus, they did not know. Crucially, Collins and Pinch *never* explain the outcome of the debate – the consensus that cold nuclear fusion did not occur – by citing the fact that it really did not occur. Truth and falsity are treated alike. '[W]e are perfectly happy to accept the truth we are given [when controversy evolves into consensus] once we finish our studies, but this is not the same as basing our studies upon it' (ibid: 175). They accept realism about physical facts only when *not* engaged in the social history of science. While doing that, they accept social realism – realism about sociological explanatory factors – but reject natural realism. Whether or not they would accept the label, I will call this approach a 'debunking account' because it tends to undermine the scientific status of natural scientific claims.

On a debunking social history of science approach, historical explanation concerns the social and political organisation of competing laboratories and how some were better able to publicise their views, eventually shutting out those of their competitors. Hence, in this example, the debate came to an end with the claims about nuclear fusion that are now accepted: it is not possible under everyday conditions. Our beliefs about the relevant physical facts are thus explained using those earlier social factors, hence the label social 'constructionism'.

On a non-debunking or vindicatory account, all of the social-historical explanatory claims previously set out may be true but there is also a further explanatory fact in addition to them. It is explanatory to say: cold nuclear fusion is, in fact, impossible. That physical fact stands at the start of all sorts of evidential chains. It explains why the experiments that seemed to suggest it was possible were not replicated. (Why some seemed to show it to be possible becomes a pressing matter although Collins and Pinch also do a good job of explaining much of this.) A vindicatory social-historical account is an explanation of the social factors that enabled a physical or natural scientific fact to *come into view*.

What makes a debunking or social constructionist account debunking is that physical or natural scientific facts are not deployed to explain our beliefs about them. The explanation runs the other way. The *explanans* are social historical, not physical or natural scientific. Hence, the analysis accords physical facts merely derivative status. Whether the debunking account assumes that there are no independent physical facts or whether it merely eschews them in the explanation of our beliefs about them is not always clear. The previous quotation from Collins and Pinch, for example, implies that agnosticism about independent physical facts is recommended only while carrying out a social-historical analysis of natural science.

Foucault's and Davidson's approach to the history of mental illness is debunking. According to them, the proper explanation of the increase in diagnosis and treatment of mental illnesses is not a greater understanding of pre-existing conditions. Rather, the locution 'there really is such an illness' is given what limited truth it has by the social-historical story about the rise of capitalism.

This stark contrast between debunking and non-debunking social-historical accounts of natural science is made more complex by the caveat mentioned previously: that there must be *some* behavioural and experiential differences that serve as the prompting for the ascription 'mental illness'. On a debunking account, there is a mismatch between the existing differences as described in the social-historical account and the medical psychiatric kinds ascribed. On the vindicatory account, the social-historical account explains how sensitivity to underlying biomedical pathology, correctly reflected in the ascribed psychiatric kinds, came about.

This is the background to Hacking's account of what he first calls 'looping' kinds. He attempts to offer a middle ground between a vindicatory and a debunking story. Looping kinds stand in contrast to natural kinds. In *The Social Construction of What?* much the same contrast is made using 'interactive kinds' and 'indifferent kinds' (Hacking 1999). Looping or interactive kinds are meant to be less objective than natural kinds. They inherit *something* of the debunking story. At the same time, they are still supposed to be *real*.

Why Looping or Interactive?

Why 'looping' or 'interactive'? Because, according to Hacking, the existence of a label directly affects those subjects who fall under it.

> 'Interactive' is a new concept that applies not to people but classifications ... that can influence what is classified ... We are especially concerned with classifications that, when known by people or those around them, and put to work in institutions, change the ways in which individuals experience themselves – and may even lead people to evolve their feelings and behavior in part because they are so classified. (Hacking 1999: 103–4)

In the paper 'Making up people', Hacking claims that the very existence of such a kind can make people into people of that kind. One example is multiple personality disorder (MPD).

> I claim that multiple personality as an idea and as a clinical phenomenon was invented around 1875: only one or two possible cases per generation had been recorded before that time, but a whole flock of them came after.
>
> (Hacking 1991: 162)

The existence of the diagnosis MPD, for example, has an effect on people in such a way as to make people fit the diagnosis. Hacking does not offer a clear a priori account of looping kinds. He says:

> I do not think that there is a general story to be told about making up people. Each category has its own history (Hacking 1991: 168)

But the nature of the looping is something like this:

(1) Introduction of the concept of multiple personality along with the associated label.
(2) Certain people are classified as having multiple personality or as falling under that kind and are treated accordingly.
(3) Some of these people come to identify with the kind multiple personality (whether consciously or not).
(4) These people (or some of them) become further distinguished from other people, often acquiring new properties.
(5) The kind multiple personality comes to be associated with a new set of properties, which leads us to modify our concept of multiple personality or the theoretical beliefs associated with it. (Khalidi 2010: 337)

This does not yet clearly indicate the metaphysical status of looping or interactive kinds. The latter is initially contrasted with what Hacking calls 'indifferent kinds' that are non-looping and look to be natural kinds. But he also offers an analogy with the historic philosophical debate between realists and nominalists (see Section 4).

> If there were some truth in the descriptions I and others have furnished, then making up people would bear on one of the great traditional questions of philosophy, namely, the debate between nominalists and realists ... You will recall that a traditional nominalist says that stars (or algae, or justice) have nothing in common except our names ('stars', 'algae', 'justice'). The traditional realist in contrast finds it amazing that the world could so kindly sort itself into our categories. He protests that there are definite sorts of objects in it, at least stars and algae, which we have painstakingly come to recognize and classify correctly.
>
> (Hacking 1991: 164)

Rejecting nominalism as true of *all* classifications, Hacking suggests that looping kinds are a form of local – rather than universal – dynamic nominalism: 'numerous human beings and human acts come into being hand in hand with our invention of categories labelling them' (ibid: 170). This suggests that looping kinds stand in some sort of contrast to natural kinds, connected to the idea that the human classifications 'make up' people. If psychiatric kinds are looping kinds, then that would suggest a contrast with the kinds in natural science but without presupposing the truth of full-blown debunking social constructionism.

Are Looping or Interactive Kinds Distinct from Natural Kinds?

Despite both the intuitive attraction of looping or interactive kinds and the various historical accounts Hacking offers using this notion, I do not think it serves as a plausible way to shed light on psychiatric kinds.

First, there can be feedback effects on the things that instantiate what seem plausible to constitute natural kinds (Bogen 1988; Cooper 2004). As Cooper argues: 'the characteristics of domestic livestock change over time because particular animals are classified as being the "Best in Show" and are used in selective breeding – sheep and pigs would now look very different if it weren't for our classificatory practices' (Cooper 2004: 78). But nothing significant seems to follow for the nature or status of such a kind from the fact that the entities to which it applies come to change as a result of being so classified. Bringing about change does not seem to be sufficient to mark out a significant difference in categories.

The key question this suggests is thus how such feedback occurs for looping kinds. Is there something significant about the route to change for looping but not for such biological kinds as species of livestock?

The clearest suggestion Hacking makes contrasts cases such as Cooper's, which depend on human interference with the non-human realm, with cases where what we do is linked to a certain description, following Elizabeth Anscombe's account of action (Anscombe 2000).

> Except when we interfere, what things are doing ... does not depend on how we describe them. But some of the things that we ourselves do are intimately connected to our descriptions. Many philosophers follow Elizabeth Anscombe and say that intentional human actions must be 'actions under a description'. ... [I]f a description is not there, then intentional actions under that description cannot be there either. (Hacking 1991: 166)

Anscombe stresses the idea that an action is the action it is in virtue of the description under which it falls. Consider an example suggested by the later philosopher of action Donald Davidson. 'A man moves his finger, let us say intentionally, thus flicking the switch, causing a light to come on, the room to be illuminated, and a prowler to be alerted'. (Davidson 1980: 53)

In the example, flicking the switch, turning on the light, and illuminating the room are all intentional. They are appropriate descriptions of the man's action. But, without knowing it, he has also alerted the prowler. But, while he *did* that, it was not his action. Thoughts of the prowler played no role in his motivation. On Anscombe's account, actions are constituted by the descriptions under which they fall.

Having a way to think about the world opens up possibilities of action. A cat could never intentionally turn on a light. Only those who know the rules of football can attempt to avoid an offside trap. Knowing the rules opens up a space of possible actions. So one way a kind might 'loop' is by introducing social rules. Given the category MPD, for example, an actor can now *act* having MPD.

This idea can also generate a different distinction to Hacking's, instead following Peter Winch, between natural and human kinds (Winch [1958] 1990). The rules that govern social interaction, unlike physical laws, are known and intentionally followed by those they govern, who thus act in accord with their own conception of the rules. Billiard balls, by contrast, do not intentionally follow the laws of Newtonian mechanics. So social 'science' is, at the very least, different from natural science. (Winch argues this disbars the very idea of social *science*.)

But this idea does not fit the cases of looping Hacking mentions in which it is not so much that new ways of acting are proposed by new social and linguistic rules, in the way that players might adapt to a new version of the offside rule. The phenomena Hacking discusses seem less self-conscious. He says 'People spontaneously come to fit their categories' (Hacking 1991: 161). This seems more like a subconscious placebo or perhaps nocebo, especially in his comment that classifications may lead people to evolve their feelings and behaviour because they are so classified (Hacking 1999: 104). An Anscombian account of action sheds light on what it would be to *act as if* one had MPD but would not itself explain why more people would choose to 'play' by these rules.

Without the link to action explanation, however, then the idea that the existence of natural classifications can lead to changes in the entities they pick out lacks any particular metaphysical significance. It thus undermines the very idea of looping or interactive kinds. Change alone does not mark out looping kinds from biological kinds such as species. But change essentially connected to the notion of the constitution of actions, which fits

Anscombe and Winch, is too narrow to account for the phenomena Hacking highlights.

There is one further complicating factor. In *The Social Construction of What?* Hacking attempts to perform a shotgun wedding of looping or interactive kinds and natural or indifferent kinds (Hacking 1999). He suggests that the looping kinds of mental illnesses might be found a posteriori to be neurological kinds in the way that water was found to be a chemical kind, H_2O. While the 'stereotype' for a kind might be looping, its underlying nature might have an essence. Hilary Putnam proposed an account of stereotypes as descriptions of the typical features of categories used to recognise them. A stereotype might be the visual appearance of a kind, described independently of its underlying essential features, although those features might also explain the stereotypical properties. For gold, the stereotype might comprise colour, malleability, and so forth. Hacking suggests that the stereotype for mental illnesses might loop, while there might still be an underlying non-looping nature. It seems that his aim is to show how looping kinds can still be *real* kinds. But it is far from clear what remains of the notion of a non-natural looping kind once it is tied even more closely than MPC kinds (Section 4) to an underlying essence.

Summary

What makes a debunking sociological account debunking is that natural facts never explain; they are always explained by social facts. Hacking's account attempts to avoid choosing between a vindicatory history of psychiatry, in which mental illnesses were discovered by mainly nineteenth-century German psychiatrists and a Foucauldian sceptical story, in which the same illnesses were 'made up' to serve some other social purposes. But it is not clear how the idea of a looping kind achieves this balance, nor what the metaphysical significance of looping itself is.

Section 6 will examine a different contrast with more familiar natural kinds: the idea that mental illnesses might be real but local rather than universal. In the conclusion, I will return to the motivation for a debunking account of mental illness explored in this section.

6 Transcultural Psychiatry and Cultural Concepts of Distress

The previous section examined Ian Hacking's attempt to articulate a general reason why psychiatric diagnostic kinds might have a principled difference from natural kinds. He argues that they 'loop' or interact with the human subjects whom they classify. But, I argued, it is not clear how the interactions that create looping kinds differ from other kinds of and hence what its general significance is for the objectivity or validity of psychiatric kinds.

This section will examine a different reason for thinking that psychiatric kinds may have a distinct status from the kinds found in physical medicine. Physical illnesses are universal in this sense: although their rates may vary geographically, the nature of the illnesses does not.

There are examples of what look like niche specific physical illnesses. 'Phossy jaw' was an occupational hazard of people who worked in the match-stick industry in the nineteenth and early twentieth centuries and is now, fortunately, rare. It is, nevertheless, universal in this sense: anyone suitably exposed is liable to suffer from phosphorous necrosis. The causal conditions may be local and culturally determined by social and economic factors but the constitution of the illness is universal.

Transcultural psychiatry, however, suggests that mental illnesses may not be universal in this sense. The nature and the possibilities of illnesses themselves may vary from culture to culture. And hence, there may be genuine, but merely local, illnesses. This section will examine whether this is a cogent possibility and, if so, how.

In the next part, I will set out the way in which *DSM-IV* and *DSM-5* (the title changed from Roman to Arabic numerals) have addressed cultural factors in part through the description of cultural concepts and idioms of distress and guidance on cultural 'formulations'. In the subsequent part, I will examine an influential picture of the role of culture in shaping mental illnesses in a two-factor model comprising 'pathogenic' and 'pathoplastic' aspects. This suggests the possibility of three possible models: the two-factor model just mentioned and two single-factor models. In the final part of the section, I will use these to examine whether there could be genuine but local mental illnesses and whether the examples given in the *DSM* might suggest how. I will argue that there could be but that the approach taken by the *DSM* is unlikely to account for them satisfactorily.

Cultural Factors in *DSM-5*

The fourth edition of the *DSM* introduced guidelines for a 'cultural formulation' and a 'Glossary of Culture-Bound Syndromes' (APA 1994). The cultural formulation supplemented the main general diagnostic criteria with a description emphasising the patient's personal experiences and their cultural reference group. The 'culture-bound syndromes' were described as 'locality-specific patterns of aberrant behavior and troubling experience that may or may not be linked to a particular *DSM-IV* diagnostic category' (APA 2000: 898).

These new elements in the *DSM* reflected the need for it to address growing cultural diversity within America since '[i]mmigrants bring with them their own indigenous patterns and conceptions of mental illness, some of which are structured into cultural syndromes' (Guarnaccia and Rogler 1999: 1322). In addition, the *DSM* needed to contain cross-cultural material because of its increasing global use.

DSM-5 offers a more extended treatment of cultural factors (APA 2013). The Introduction warns how cultural factors might affect diagnosis and prognosis and thus should be investigated in a cultural formulation. Diagnostic criteria were revised to reflect cross-cultural variations in how disorders manifest themselves. The 'Cultural Formulation' includes a semi-structured interview. There is a 'Glossary of Cultural Concepts of Distress' that describes nine common conditions.

The Introduction also summarises (in fact at greater length than the later discussion of the cultural formulation in the main text) three distinct ways that culture can impact diagnoses (APA 2013). The single idea of culture-bound syndromes from *DSM-IV* is replaced by three notions: cultural syndromes, cultural idioms of distress, and cultural explanations (or perceived causes) of illnesses (or symptoms).

1. *Cultural syndrome* is a cluster or group of co-occurring, relatively invariant symptoms found in a specific cultural group . . ..
2. *Cultural idiom of distress* is a linguistic term, phrase, or way of talking about suffering among individuals of a cultural group . . ..
3. *Cultural explanation or perceived cause* is a label, attribution, or feature of an explanatory model that provides a culturally conceived etiology or cause for symptoms, illness, or distress . . .. (ibid: 14)

The same elements may play a role in all three categories. For example, *depression* is used as an idiom of distress whether of an illness or of normal but significant sadness. But it is also recognised as a mental illness syndrome gathering together a number of symptoms. Finally, it is taken to be the cause of those symptoms. Just as depression can play the role of the syndrome, idiom of distress, and explanation, so can other concepts local to other cultures.

Given this complication, although the 'Glossary of Cultural Concepts of Distress' describes nine common cultural syndromes, the concepts described may also play a role as idioms of distress and purported explanations or causes of experiences. The 'Cultural Concepts of Distress' described are *khyal* attacks or *khyal cap, ataque de nervios* ('attack of nerves'), *dhat* ('semen loss'), *kufungisisa* ('thinking too much' in Shona), *maladi moun* ('humanly caused illness') *nervios* ('nerves'), *shenjing shuairuo* ('weakness of the nervous system' in Mandarin Chinese), *susto* ('fright'), and *taijin kyofusho* ('interpersonal fear disorder' in Japanese). Each is related to similar but different concepts found in other cultures and also to the categories set out in the main body of *DSM-5*. *Khyal cap*, for example, is linked to panic disorder.

In the rest of this section, I will take khyal cap as an example because I think that it is typical in the underlying structure of all the conditions listed. (This is an assumption: I leave it to the reader to consider its plausibility by studying the descriptions in the *DSM* glossary.) It is described thus.

Khyal Cap

'*Khyal* attacks' *(khyal cap)*, or 'wind attacks', is a syndrome found among Cambodians in the United States and Cambodia. Common symptoms include those of panic attacks, such as dizziness, palpitations, shortness of breath, and cold extremities, as well as other symptoms of anxiety and autonomic arousal (e.g., tinnitus and neck soreness). *Khyal* attacks include catastrophic cognitions centered on the concern that *khyal* (a windlike substance) may rise in the body – along with blood – and cause a range of serious effects (e.g., compressing the lungs to cause shortness of breath and asphyxia; entering the cranium to cause tinnitus, dizziness, blurry vision, and a fatal syncope). *Khyal* attacks may occur without warning, but are frequently brought about by triggers such as worrisome thoughts, standing up (i.e., orthostasis), specific odors with negative associations, and agoraphobic type cues like going to crowded spaces or riding in a car. *Khyal* attacks usually meet panic attack criteria and may shape the experience of other anxiety and trauma- and stress or related disorders. *Khyal* attacks may be associated with considerable disability.

Related conditions in other cultural contexts: Laos *(pen lom)*, Tibet *(srog rlunggi nad)*, Sri Lanka *(vata)*, and Korea *(hwa byung)*.

Related conditions in DSM-5: Panic attack, panic disorder, generalized anxiety disorder, agoraphobia, posttraumatic stress disorder, illness anxiety disorder. (ibid: 834)

The belief that illness can be caused by a dysfunction of a wind-like substance seems to be common in parts of Asia (Hinton *et al.* 2010: 245). Khyal is thought normally to flow alongside the blood supply and can pass out of the body through the skin. But the flow can become disturbed 'surging upward in the body toward the head, often accompanied by blood, to cause many symptoms and possibly various bodily disasters' (ibid: 245). It is thought to be caused by, for example, 'worry, standing up, a change in the weather and any kind of fright, such as being startled or awakening from a nightmare' (ibid: 246). Local treatments include dragging a coin along the skin giving rise to characteristic abrasions.

Khyal attack is a good example because it is very clear that the framework of beliefs that surround the conception of khyal attack differs from that of biomedical psychiatry. It *looks* culturally relative. At the same time, its status as a genuine illness is supported in the *DSM*, despite its position merely in a glossary, by links to other diagnostic categories from the main body of the text. And hence it may count as a genuine but local mental illness.

Does it? And what is its supposed status in *DSM-5*? These questions call for a general understanding of the ways in which culture might affect concepts of illness and whether any model can simultaneously aim for objectivity or validity whilst admitting cultural variation. Thus, the next part will outline three general ways of thinking about the cultural dependence of mental illness categories, the possible role of cultural formulations, and hence the different cultural concepts of distress in *DSM-5*.

Three Models of Cultural Concepts of Distress

A Two-Factor Pathogenic-Pathoplastic Model

One way to understand how culture affects mental illness is to think of the *expression* of mental illness as the result of two factors: an invariant endogenous factor and a local cultural appearance. The German psychiatrist Karl Birnbaum called the first component 'pathogenic' and the second 'pathoplastic' (Birnbaum [1923] 1974). The psychiatrist and anthropologist Roland Littlewood emphasises the connection between this distinction and the long-standing distinction in psychiatry between the form and content of mental illnesses.

> To deal with variations in the symptoms between individuals, while maintain-
> ing the idea of a uniform disease, clinical psychiatry still makes a distinction
> between the essential *pathogenic* determinants of a mental disorder – those
> biological processes which are held to be necessary and sufficient to cause it –
> and the *pathoplastic* personal and cultural variations in the pattern. Those two
> are still distinguished in everyday clinical practice by the particularly nine-
> teenth century German distinction between form and content.
>
> (Littlewood 2002: 5)

Littlewood reports that on the standard picture, the first, pathogenic factor is a biological process. Against a background biomedical view of psychiatry, that is the most obvious interpretation. Furthermore, it fits an influential analysis of the nature of the mental disorder in general. As I described in Section 3, Jerome Wakefield argues that a mental or physical disorder is a harmful biological dysfunction where the notion of function and dysfunction is explained by appeal to evolutionary theory (Wakefield 1999). Hence, it might seem natural to think of the pathogenic factor not just as a biological process but also more specifically as a biological *dysfunction*.

Cultural variation enters this (two-factor) picture only with the second, pathoplastic factor. Culturally invariant pathologies of underlying human nature are overlaid by cultural variation in expression. 'Expression' could merely mean that standing possibilities for biological dysfunction might be differently caused in different cultural contexts, akin to variation in heart disease rates in different societies. The more interesting idea is that variation in 'expression' picks out the way in which underlying pathologies might be shaped by the different self-interpretations in different cultures and thus the way the pathologies are experienced and avowed. This would be an example of a cultural *idiom* of distress in the vocabulary of the *DSM-5*. But, whereas for physical illness, how one understands one's illness might be an accidental superficiality compared with the real underlying condition, one might argue that for mental illness, its *esse* is *percipi*: how it is perceived at least partly constitutes what it is.

One might think, for example, that *khyal cap* and panic disorder have the same underlying biological mechanism but that the characteristic way in which the former carries its own ontology (i.e., that subjects think of their distress through the conceptual lens of a dysfunction of the flow of wind-like substance) is sufficient to mark it off as a different kind of mental illness from the latter. Biological dysfunction is then the common *cause* of two *distinct* illnesses depending on cultural context. On the other hand, one might think that the real illness is whatever is common to *khyal cap* and panic disorder: the pathogenic cause. It is merely that the appearance that this single illness takes can vary.

Whichever view is taken of whether the pathogenic factor is the illness or merely the common underpinning of different illnesses, a two-factor pathogenic-pathoplastic view of cultural concepts of mental illness suggests a particular view of the aim of a cultural formulation in psychiatric diagnosis. It is a way of inferring, from locally divergent symptoms, the common underlying nature, or the underlying causes, of mental illness. The aim of sensitivity to cultural difference would be to find a way to penetrate beneath it to a common substrate appropriate for scientific psychiatric research.

This seems to be the view of the ex-president of the World Psychiatric Association, Juan Mezzich, and his co-authors in their discussion of 'Cultural formulation guidelines' when they say:

> Performing a cultural formulation of illness requires of the clinician to translate the patient's information about self, social situation, health, and

> illness into a general biopsychosocial framework that the clinician uses to
> organize diagnostic assessment and therapeutics. In effect, the clinician seeks
> to map what he or she has learned about the patient's illness onto the
> conceptual framework of clinical psychiatry.   (Mezzich *et al.* 2009: 391)

The previous passages suggest that there is a division between how an illness is
expressed and the underlying framework set out by biomedical psychiatry. The
former is locally culturally shaped. The latter is invariant. On Mezzich *et al*'s
account, the only positive role cultural factors can then play is as a source of
contingent health-promoting resources:

> The aim is to summarize how culturally salient themes can be used to enhance
> care and health promotion strategies (e.g., involvement of the patient's
> family, utilization of helpful cultural values). (ibid: 399)

'Culturally salient themes' do not reveal the shape of mental illnesses in
themselves but can, contingently, be used to promote health because of their
effects on how people understand their own illnesses. This implies a two-factor
view, which is one of three possible views. I will argue that it is a halfway house
between two more radical views of the possibilities for cultural psychiatry,
which I will now outline.

Two Single-Factor Models of Cultural Variation: Pathoplastic-Only and Pathogenic-Only

A two-factor model of the nature of transcultural psychiatry requires
a distinction between surface appearance and underlying pathology. But it
might be that this distinction cannot be drawn.

Consider, again, the idea that the pathogenic factor is a biological dysfunction. Drawing a distinction between this and the surface appearance of an illness
might seem unproblematic for some illnesses. It requires that a common underlying biological dysfunction can be identified despite different culturally
imposed behaviours or experiences. But, in the case of some mental dysfunctions, there may be no principled way of drawing a distinction between an
underlying function and the surface appearance.

As well as on social, cultural, and educational factors, human minds depend
on the nature of human brains. Thus, there may be shared biological processes
underpinning different culturally shaped experiences of mental illness. But one
cannot treat just any shared biological process as the first factor of a *mental*
illness. The biological process has to be a *mental* process: a failure of a mental
function (Graham 2010: 24, 2013). It is thus less clear that there must be *shared*
mental dysfunctions between different experiences. The dysfunction may be
located only at the surface, mental level. (This is not to say that mental states

cannot be brain states. But, just as software failures may reveal no failure at the hardware level, mental illness has to comprise a dysfunction at the mental level.)

Suppose that human nature can be divided between our biological natures and what the philosopher John McDowell calls 'second nature' or, in German, *Bildung* (McDowell 1994: 183). Our second nature has to be developed through education and enculturation. A good example is an initiation into a first language and an inherited world view. Whilst the ability to develop a second nature is contingent on biological first nature, that biology is insufficient for it.

So positing physical-biological processes as the pathogenic factor looks to be at the wrong level for a *mental* illness of second nature. But, if instead one talks of mental processes, it is unclear how in general to distinguish between the surface appearance of mental illness, its characteristic experiences for example, and an underlying and yet still mental process. Mental illness – or some mental illnesses – may be essentially features of the surface appearance of our second nature.

If the distinction between the two levels on which the two-factor pathogenic-pathoplastic model depends cannot be drawn for at least some mental illnesses, that leaves only one factor. There are, however, two possible one-factor models depending on whether one thinks that apparent variation in mental illness is either all pathogenic or all pathoplastic.

A pathogenic-only model holds that illness varies only in external features such as rates and merely superficial local understandings of it. Any apparently deeper variation would be a mark of our ignorance, our misdiagnosis. Thus, a pathogenic-only model has no need for a cultural formulation to extract or excavate the underlying commonalities because they are open to view.

But it is also possible that because second nature depends on enculturation and because cultures vary, human second nature also varies. If so, the richer notion of human nature, beyond mere biology and sufficient for a conception of mental illness, might be local rather than universal. Cultural variation might go 'all the way down'. Genuinely different forms of mental illness would *emerge* from different ways of living in different societies. This is the pathoplastic-only model.

The pathoplastic-only model is more radical than the two-factor model even though both agree on the need for some sort of cultural formulation. A pathoplastic-only version of a cultural formulation is more radical because it does not enable one to dig beneath surface difference to find underlying common pathologies but would instead be an articulation of the genuinely different ways people can be ill in different cultures. According to it, there are genuinely different forms of mental illness that have nothing substantial in common across different cultures. The correctness or validity of a psychiatric taxonomy and its universality diverge.

In fact, sympathy for a pathoplastic-only view of mental illness sometimes seems to go hand in hand with a view that questions the *illness* status of cultural idioms of distress. For example, Littlewood offers an anthropological insight into female overdosing in Anglo-American society via a comparison with the behavioural patterns of women in 'less pluralistic small-scale societies', looking 'not just at the person involved but at the local meaning of the act in the political context in which it happens' (Littlewood 2002: 36). In so doing, he offers an anthropological understanding by sketching the social *function* of behaviour in society rather than an individual *pathology* or dysfunction. It may be that the pathoplastic-only model requires an anthropological stance and that such a stance will look for and often find social order rather than individual illness or disorder. But, I will suggest later in the text, that is not an essential feature of a pathoplastic-only approach. There is nothing inconsistent with the idea that a pathoplastic-only model is a model of illness.

The Status of Khyal Cap

I proposed at the start of this section that transcultural psychiatry may suggest that mental illness can be culturally relative rather than universal. The nature and possible forms of illnesses themselves may vary from culture to culture, as well as their rates and risks. And hence there may be genuine but merely local illnesses. This prompts a second question: does *DSM-5*'s 'Glossary of Cultural Concepts of Distress' suggest any candidates for such local illnesses? The previous part examined three possible general models of mental illness relevant to transcultural psychiatry: pathogenic-pathoplastic, plathogenic-only, and pathoplastic-only. In this part, I will consider the example of *khyal* attack to see if qualifies as a genuine local illness under one or more of the three models.

Recall Mezzich *et al*'s suggestion that the role of a cultural formulation is to 'map what he or she has learned about the patient's illness onto the conceptual framework of clinical psychiatry'. This reflects an implicit two-factor pathogenic-pathoplastic model. Given the description in *DSM-5*, it seems plausible that the underlying invariant pathogenic factor is whatever is common to *khyal* attack and the other related conditions *DSM-5* lists: 'panic attack, panic disorder, generalised anxiety disorder, agoraphobia, posttraumatic stress disorder, [or] illness anxiety disorder' (APA 2013: 834). The varying local cultural shape, the pathoplastic factor, is the local features specifically of *khyal* attack not shared by those other conditions: that is 'catastrophic cognitions centered on the concern that *khyal* (a wind-like substance) may rise in the body'.

Khyal attack thus seems to fit the two-factor model dating back to nineteenth-century German psychiatry. But fitting *khyal* attack into the model does not quite provide an example of the target idea of this section – a genuine but merely local illness – because there remains an asymmetry between it and panic attack, for example. From the perspective of the rest of the *DSM*, the former, but not the latter, involves an error about the aetiology of the condition. On the assumption that human physiology does not involve a wind-like substance, the description of *khyal* attack involves a mistaken idea as to its aetiology because the local understanding of its nature partly comprises the condition. Whatever the sufferer thinks, there is no rising up of a wind-like substance going on. And hence, it fits the characterisation that Littlewood critically offers of *traditional* transcultural psychiatry, namely, that it charts the *errors* of non-Western approaches to illness. Insofar as the 'Glossary of Cultural Concepts of Distress' comprises 'illnesses', a form of insincerity or irony attaches to the judgement that they really are so.

Could *khyal* attack be fitted to a pathogenic-only model? That model presents a stark choice for any putative newly discovered mental illness. Cultural syndromes such as *khyal cap* can have either of two statuses. They are either really other names for universal conditions also picked out by the vocabulary of biomedical psychiatry such as 'panic disorder'. Or they do not exist. For example, if it is an essential part of the theoretical apparatus of *khyal cap* that it is caused by the rising up of a wind-like substance, then, given that on our best account of physiology, there is no such substance, there is no such condition. Those who self-report it, or its characteristic symptoms, are in some sense in error about their own condition. Predictably, given its universalist assumption, a pathogenic-only approach provides no support for the idea of local but genuine mental illnesses.

This leaves the pathoplastic-only model. Can it underpin the plausibility of genuine but local illnesses, and does *DSM-5*'s 'Glossary of Cultural Concepts of Distress' suggest any candidates?

In rejecting the traditional two-factor model of transcultural psychiatry, anthropologically minded psychiatrists such as Roland Littlewood and Arthur Kleinman, have implicitly favoured a pathoplastic-only model (e.g., Littlewood 1985, 1986, 2002). '[C]ulture-bound syndromes are representations in the individual of symbolic themes concerning social relations and which occur in certain personal and historical situations. They articulate both personal predicament and public'. (Littlewood 1985: 704)

This passage sketches the idea of a pathology of human second nature constituted by local personal and historical situations with no attempt to identify a universal pathogenic foundation. Such a view, however, also plays down the illness or pathological status of the behaviour. It emphasises instead its positive social function in addressing, in the case sketched, an imbalance of power. In his paper 'The culture-bound syndromes of the dominant culture', Littlewood applies the same style of analysis to diagnoses found in the *main* sections of *DSM*. Agoraphobia, for example, is argued to serve an adaptive function for a woman against her husband without open defiance, binding them both together at home (Littlewood and Lipsedge 1986: 262–3).

So it might seem that a pathoplastic-only approach can address a worry about the asymmetric treatment of syndromes in the main body of the *DSM* and the appendix that otherwise threatens the target idea that local forms of mental illness are as genuine as the supposedly universal forms codified in the main body the *DSM* text. If the same pathoplastic-only approach is taken to the syndromes set out in the rest of *DSM-5*, then it seems that those in the 'Glossary of Cultural Concepts of Distress' have the same status. They are no less genuine forms of illness.

But there is a cost to this. It is not that an ironic attitude to the cultural concepts of distress is avoided. It is, rather, that it is generalised to include diagnoses of supposedly genuine illnesses in the main body of the *DSM* text such as agoraphobia and anorexia nervosa because their status as pathological is undermined by construing them as culturally relative forms of social *function* rather than *dysfunction*.

Furthermore, debunking psychiatric syndromes set out in the main body of the *DSM* by arguing that they are really meaning-laden adaptive strategies rather than genuine pathologies may be plausible in some cases (perhaps ADHD, personality disorder, depression following bereavement). But it seems implausible across the board. A globally ironic attitude to every mental illness syndrome is a high price to pay for affording cultural concepts equal status.

But a pathoplastic-only approach need not deny the pathological status of conditions nor take a debunking attitude to claims of local pathology. It could be taken to chart genuinely different ways of being ill resulting from being in a different culture. This requires adopting some sort of universal concept of illness, as discussed in earlier sections, but one that can take culturally relative forms. Adopting a cross-cultural model of *illness* with local variations in how it is realised is no more problematic in principle than adopting a cross-cultural model of socially *adaptive functions* with local variations in realisation, as Littlewood appears to do.

Not all general analyses of illness fit well with the idea of a pathoplastic approach, however. Wakefield's analysis, for example, presupposes biological dysfunction as explained by human evolutionary history. Such an apparently universalist notion cannot easily be made to fit with a pathoplastic-only contemporary variation. As sketched earlier, it fits better with a two-factor model. But Bill Fulford's failure of ordinary doing account does seem consistent with a pathoplastic approach. It might be that there are local standards for what counts as ordinary doing and hence novel possibilities for endogenously caused failures of such doing, amounting to illness on this approach. Identifying such failures of action would require anthropological understanding of the culture and might produce interesting variations between cultures. Behaviour that amounts to agoraphobia in the UK might involve no failure of ordinary doing in a culture in which a subpopulation is not expected to venture outside, in monastic communities, perhaps.

Despite the possibility of a pathoplastic-only approach to local conceptions of pathology (rather than socially adaptive functions), this does not help in the case of *khyal cap*, and hence, I suggest the other examples from *DSM-5*'s 'Glossary of Cultural Concepts of Distress', which share its form. The problem is that it involves not just a description of a local failure of function or action. In fact, the possibility of construing it as a variant of a panic attack or disorder suggests a continuity of the kind of dysfunction or failure of action that it embodies with those recognised in the main body of the *DSM*. Rather, the main difference lies within the local aetiological theory. But this is not merely different from, but rather incompatible with, the view of the body contained within biomedical psychiatry. Espousing both a traditional psychiatric view in the main body of the text and an incompatible view in the glossary threatens the validity of one or the other. They cannot both be set out as true accounts.

Summary

This section has addressed two questions. Is there a plausible model of genuine but non-universal, culturally relative mental illnesses, and does *DSM-5*'s 'Glossary of Cultural Concepts of Distress' suggest any candidates? The history of transcultural psychiatry offers the two-factor model of mental illness as comprising both a universal pathogenic element and a local pathoplastic shaping. This, in turn, suggests the logical possibility, at least, of pathogenic-only and pathoplastic-only models.

If illness comprises only a pathogenic component, then there is no possibility of significant or deep cultural variation: merely variation of superficial features such as rate. The two-factor model is more promising. Furthermore, it is consistent, at least, with Wakefield's influential harmful dysfunction model of illness. But there are at least two difficulties with using it as a general model of genuine but local forms of illness. First, it runs the risk of falling prey to Littlewood's charge of amounting merely to an error account. As the example of khyal attack illustrates, there is a danger that the cultural shaping is a local false account of aetiology. That suggests that the real illness is not the combination of both factors but merely the pathogenic core. In other words, there is a tendency for this model to collapse into the pathogenic-only model, construing cultural variation as a merely medically insignificant cosmetic appearance.

Second, and more fundamentally, there may be principled difficulties in separating the pathoplastic from the pathogenic, given that that pathogenic factor of a mental illness must itself be mental. That is not to deny that mental illness can have a multiplicity of *causal* factors, both mental and physical, local and distant, including social causes. But if the two-factor account is supposed to explain the cultural variation of what *comprises* mental illness, both factors need to be characterised in mental terms. It is not clear, however, that such a distinction is *generally* possible.

Hence, the most promising way to articulate genuine but local forms of mental illness is via a pathoplastic-only approach. I have suggested that these comprise illnesses of human second nature. Such an approach is also consistent with Fulford's account of illness as a failure of ordinary doing, which in turn suggests one way that there could be such illnesses. Cultural practices constitute local forms of action and hence set local standards for ordinary doing. This reflects the discussion in the previous section of how Anscombe's account of action could have helped Hacking's account of looping kinds. Actions are constituted as the actions they are through the intentions of those who undertake them. Such intentions are made possible by social rules. Only if the game of rugby exists is it possible to attempt to score a try, or actually score one. Only given rules governing linguistic representation is it possible to attempt to read and write. Hence, new forms of ordinary doing open up new possibilities of pathoplastic-only mental illnesses. The institution of reading and writing, for example, is presupposed by the idea of dyslexia being an illness on this view (contrast the discussion of Wakefield and dyslexia in Section 3).

The coherence of a pathoplastic-only view of mental illness suggests, at best, that there *could* be genuine but culturally relative mental illnesses. Whether there *are* any and if so how many is an empirical matter. But the plausibility of a role for culture in framing illnesses of second nature and the existence of illnesses – such as dyslexia – that do not easily fit an evolutionary biological view suggests that the very idea of mental illness permits a kind of variability that is distinct from that of paradigmatic physical illnesses.

Conclusions

In this short work, I have explored two opposing general intuitions about mental illness. One takes the various dissimilarities between mental illnesses and paradigmatic physical illnesses to be a reason to deny the former illness status. The other holds that there are sufficient underlying similarities, despite the apparent differences, for mental illnesses properly to count as illnesses. The former view denies particular illness kinds a real, objective, or natural status. The latter holds that while not essentialist kinds, the sort that seems to fit chemistry, they could be genuine, objective, or natural kinds of a more relaxed form such as MPCs, in which the tying together of stable properties in law-like ways helps sustain inductive generalisations for explanation and prediction. One question that feeds into this general dispute is whether, and if so how, mental illness is value-laden. Thomas Szasz argues that it is value-laden and takes this to undermine the reality of mental illness, while, among others, both Jerome Wakefield and Bill Fulford argue, in different ways, that being value-laden is no such impediment.

What Conclusions can be drawn for the Status of Mental Illness?

I ended Section 3 with an outline of Neil Pickering's critique of what he calls the 'likeness argument'. This is a form of argument in which the features of a paradigmatic notion of illness, usually physical illness, are articulated and then equivalent features – features instancing appropriate general descriptions – are found to be present for putative mental illnesses and then used as evidence for the latter's status as genuine illnesses. Pickering argues that this fails rationally to determine the status of mental illness, or particular mental illnesses because the descriptions of the component features beg the question. Using some illustrative cases, he suggests that the component features of putative mental illnesses always permit descriptions in non-medical ways, undermining the likeness argument.

Although I argued that this was not as decisive an objection as Pickering claimed – because it undermines only an implausibly foundational interpretation of the likeness argument – it is helpful to sketch Pickering's own view of mental illness, which dovetails with his criticism of the likeness argument. He thinks that the idea that mental illness is illness is a metaphor.

The idea that mental illness incorporates a metaphorical use of 'illness' is shared by Szasz who frequently invokes it, although he less frequently explains to what it amounts.

> [T]oday, it is considered shamefully uncivilized and naively unscientific to treat a person who acts or appears sick as if he were not sick. We now 'know' and 'realize' that such a person is sick; that he is obviously sick; that he is

mentally sick. But this view rests on a serious, albeit simple, error: it rests on mistaking or confusing what is real with what is imitation; literal meaning with metaphorical meaning; medicine with morals. In other words, I maintain that mental illness is a metaphorical disease: that bodily illness stands in the same relation to mental illness as a defective television set stands to a bad television programme. Of course, the word 'sick' is often used metaphorically. We call jokes 'sick', economies 'sick', sometimes even the whole world 'sick'; but only when we call minds 'sick' do we systematically mistake and strategically misinterpret metaphor for fact – and send for the doctor to 'cure' the 'illness'. It is as if a television viewer were to send for a television engineer because he dislikes the programme he sees on the screen.

(Szasz 1973: 305–6)

Szasz takes the claim that mental illness is a metaphor to imply that it is literally false. So-called mental illnesses are not illnesses, and our calling them so is a metaphor whose metaphorical status has been forgotten. Szasz concludes that it is a form of deception.

Pickering disagrees with this conclusion. He agrees that the claim that mental illness is illness is a metaphor. It 'involves the categorization of one thing as a kind or type of thing it isn't' (Pickering 2006: 77–8). Akin to the metaphor, 'John is a wolf', 'schizophrenia is an illness' is cognitively jarring because it is a wrong categorisation. But the metaphor is often used fruitfully in science exemplified in such medical ideas as that *the body is a machine*. The body is not literally a machine, but it has proved fruitful for medicine to think of it as such.

Once a metaphor has been deployed, however, it supports claims to likenesses. Calling a heart a 'pump' licenses description of aspects of the heart as pump-like. But it is not that likenesses justify the application of the metaphor, as proponents of the likeness argument assume. Rather, the metaphor underpins the apparent likenesses. When things are contested, the likenesses are not there to be tracked and used as neutral arguments. They are constructed by the imaginative imposition of the wrong category in a metaphor.

Pickering's picture is attractive in two respects. First, it helps rationalise how the idea of calling conditions mental 'illnesses' is compatible with their dissimilarities from paradigmatic illnesses listed in Section 1. Second, it helps show how, despite that, they can share some likenesses, albeit contested, with paradigmatic illnesses. The metaphor helps suggest and hence construct these. Despite this, Pickering's picture is not persuasive.

Like the account of the likeness argument, Pickering's account of illness as metaphor looks to step back from the debate and put it in context from a loftier perspective. Defenders of mental illness such as Wakefield and Fulford deploy the likeness argument, but from Pickering's position, it seems that this should not rationally persuade their opponents, who are free to deny the subsidiary likenesses. According to Pickering, Wakefield and Fulford misunderstand their own invocation of likenesses in part because – and with echoes of the similar charge Szasz makes – they fail to grasp the fact that they have already deployed a mere metaphor on which the likenesses, to which they appeal, depend. But what is it that makes this a metaphor? Why is it that a metaphor is needed? Here, it seems that Pickering has no loftier view than his ground-level opponents. For Pickering, there is something mistaken about claiming *literally* that mental illnesses are illnesses, and hence, there is a gap to be bridged by metaphor. But, for Wakefield, for example, illnesses *just are* harmful biological dysfunctions and that applies – literally – to mental illnesses too. And thus, for Wakefield, there is no reason to think that 'illness' is the wrong name or category, nor a gap to be bridged by the creative application of the wrong word, and thus no need for a metaphor.

There is a further reason to doubt Pickering's position: it looks too strong. Suppose a novel bodily condition were discovered and the question were asked: is it an illness or just a difference? The obvious tactic for answering this would be to examine whether its subsidiary features were those of an illness: the likeness argument. But, if the application of the likeness argument *always* depends on the prior application of a metaphor, then every new application of the word 'illness' is metaphorical. Dodging this criticism by saying that it is only cognitively jarring applications that require metaphors begs the question against those who, by offering a general criterion of illness and then deploying the likeness argument, feel no cognitive jarring in the judgement, for example, that schizophrenia is an illness.

In sum, the idea that mental illness is illness merely by metaphor – even when shorn of its Szaszian pejorative connotations and thus limiting the force of the word 'merely' to contrast with a literal construal – is not satisfactory.

I have sketched Pickering's position, however, because it is at least an attempt to acknowledge that there can be rational disagreement about illness status and that it can seem a contingent matter that a number of conditions have come to be classed as illnesses. That is, it is conceivable that they might not have done. Whatever the plausibility of Michel Foucault's history, in which the idea of mental illness and its associated social practices were invented in the service of the growth of capitalism, it does seem plausible to think that the history of psychiatry might have been different. And this seems to be reflected in contemporary debates as to whether conditions such as ADHD, personality disorder, or depression following bereavement really are medical as opposed to moral, emotional, or other evaluative categories. It is also reflected in the idea that other cultures might carve up the space of possible illnesses differently, given their different cultural practices. Hence, too, the discussion of whether the diagnostic kinds currently accepted comprise natural kinds or stranger, less objective, 'looping' kinds, or whether psychiatric kinds are more plausibly located at lower levels or finer grains provide merely partial insight into the contingencies of what we call 'mental illness'.

Any reader reaching this point may feel short-changed that I have not attempted to say just what mental illness *is*: to articulate a philosophical account of it. Although pithy accounts and definitions are often a goal of philosophy, they are difficult even with concepts whose use typically commands agreement rather than a dispute in non-philosophical contexts. 'Knowledge' and 'action' are paradigmatic examples where largely unproblematic everyday use still resists non-circular philosophical analysis. The agreed extension (the class of entities to which a concept applies) seems no guarantee of an agreed philosophical account of intension (the meaning of a concept), and there can even be tension between agreed extension and philosophical accounts of intension. But mental illness is widely disputed both in its range and its meaning. Philosophical inquiry helps show some of its conceptual connections. I take it, for example, that illness is a value-laden notion, but it does not follow that the constituent values can be understood independently of, and prior to, an understanding of illness or pathology. And hence, any account of illness is likely to be circular: to presuppose the concept it was meant to explain. Nevertheless, philosophical investigation can help illuminate what is being disputed in disagreements about mental illness. It is less a matter for a semantic police force imposing the correct use and more a form of arbitration or even therapy exploring the reasons and underlying motivations of competing claims. This kind of exploration may nonetheless shed light on the nature of the complicated but very real kinds of distress to which we apply the label 'mental illness'.

Further Reading

Section 1

Bentall, R. P. (2003) *Madness explained: Psychosis and human nature*, London: Allen Lane.

Fulford, K. W. M., Davies, M., and Gipps, R. G.T., eds. (2013) *The Oxford handbook of philosophy and psychiatry*, Oxford: Oxford University Press.

Tekin, S., and Bluhm, R., eds. (2019) *The Bloomsbury companion to philosophy of psychiatry*, London: Bloomsbury.

Tsou, J. (2021) *Philosophy of psychiatry (Elements in the philosophy of science)*, Cambridge: Cambridge University Press.

Section 2

Boorse, C. (2014) A Second Rebuttal on Health. *Journal of Medicine and Philosophy* 39: 683–724.

Haldipur, C., Knoll IV, J., and vd Luft, E., eds. (2019) *Thomas Szasz: An appraisal of his legacy*, Oxford: Oxford University Press.

As well as chapters from Fulford *et al.* (2013) and Tekin and Bluhm (2019).

Section 3

Forest, D., and Faucher, L., eds. (2021) *Defining mental disorders: Jerome Wakefield and his critics*, Cambridge, MA: MIT Press.

As well as chapters from Fulford *et al.* (2013) and Tekin and Bluhm (2019).

Section 4

Davies, W., Roache, R., and Savulescu, J., eds. (2020) *Psychiatry reborn: Biopsychosocial psychiatry in modern medicine*, Oxford: Oxford University Press.

Demazeux, S. and Singy, P., eds. (2015) *The DSM-5 in perspective: Philosophical reflections on the psychiatric babel*, Dordrecht: Springer.

Kendler, K., and Parnas, J., eds. (2017) *Philosophical issues in psychiatry IV: Classification of psychiatric illness*, Oxford: Oxford University Press.

Section 5

Khalidi, M. A. (2013) *Natural categories and human kinds: Classification in the natural and social sciences*, Cambridge: Cambridge University Press.

Tsou, J. (2021) *Philosophy of psychiatry (Elements in the philosophy of science)*, Cambridge: Cambridge University Press.

Section 6

Bhugra, D., and Bhui, K., eds. (2018) *Textbook of cultural psychiatry* (2nd ed.), Cambridge: Cambridge University Press.

White, R., Read, U., Jain, S., and Orr, D., eds. (2017) *The Palgrave handbook of global mental health: Sociocultural perspectives*, London: Palgrave.

References

American Psychiatric Association (APA) (1994) *Diagnostic and statistical manual of mental disorders fourth edition (DSM-IV)*, Washington, DC: American Psychiatric Association.

American Psychiatric Association (APA) (2000) *Diagnostic and statistical manual of mental disorders fourth edition text revision (DSM-IV-TR)*, Washington, DC: American Psychiatric Association.

American Psychiatric Association (APA) (2013) *Diagnostic and statistical manual of mental disorders fifth edition (DSM-5)*, Washington, DC: American Psychiatric Association.

Anscombe, E. (2000) *Intention*, Cambridge, MA: Harvard University Press.

Austin, J. L. (1957) A plea for excuses. *Proceedings of the Aristotelian Society* 57: 1–30.

Bentall, R. P. (2003) *Madness explained: Psychosis and human nature*, London: Allen Lane.

Bhugra, D., and Bhui, K., eds. (2018) *Textbook of cultural psychiatry* (2nd ed.), Cambridge: Cambridge University Press.

Birnbaum, K. ([1923] 1974) The making of a psychosis. Translated by H. Marshall, in S. R. Hirsch and M. Shepherd, eds., *Themes and variations in European psychiatry*, Bristol: John Wright, pp. 197–238.

Bogen, J. (1988) Comments on 'The sociology of knowledge about child abuse'. *Nous* 22: 65–66.

Bolton, D. (2008) *What is mental disorder? An essay in philosophy, science and values*, Oxford: Oxford University Press.

Boorse, C. (1975) On the distinction between disease and illness. *Philosophy and Public Affairs* 5: 49–68.

Boorse, C. (1976) What a theory of mental health should be. *Journal for the Theory of Social Behaviour* 6: 61–84.

Boorse, C. (1997) A rebuttal on health. In J. M. Humber and R. F. Almeder, eds., *What is disease?* Totowa, NJ: Humana Press, pp. 1–134.

Boorse, C. (2014) A second rebuttal on health. *Journal of Medicine and Philosophy* 39: 683–724.

Boyd, R. (1991) Realism, antifoundationalism and the enthusiasm for natural kinds. *Philosophical Studies* 61: 127–48.

Campbell, J. (2009) What does rationality have to do with psychological causation? Propositional attitudes as mechanisms and as control variables. In L. Bortolotti and M. Broome, eds., *Psychiatry as cognitive neuroscience*, Oxford: Oxford University Press, pp. 137–50.

Champlin, T. S. (1989) The causation of mental illness. *Philosophical Investigations* 12: 14–32.

Charland, L. C. (2006) Moral nature of the DSM-IV Cluster B personality disorders. *Journal of Personality Disorders* 20: 116–25.

Charlson, F., van Ommeren, M., Flaxman, A. *et al.* (2019) New WHO prevalence estimates of mental disorders in conflict settings: A systematic review and meta-analysis. *The Lancet* 394:240–248. http://doi.org/10.1016/S0140-6736(19)30934-1.

Collins, H., and Pinch, T. (1998) *The golem: What you should know about science*, Cambridge: Cambridge University Press.

Cooper, R. (2004) Why hacking is wrong about human kinds. *The British Journal for the Philosophy of Science* 55: 73–85.

Cooper, R. (2007) *Psychiatry and philosophy of science*, Durham, NC: Acumen.

Cooper, R. (2013) Natural kinds. In K. W. M. Fulford, M. Davies, R. G. T. Gipps *et al.*, eds., *Oxford handbook of philosophy and psychiatry*, Oxford: Oxford University Press, pp. 950–65.

Cooper, R. (2015) Must disorders cause harm? The changing stance of the DSM. In S. Demazeux and P. Singy, eds., *The DSM-5 in perspective philosophical reflections on the psychiatric babel*, Dordrecht: Springer, pp. 83–96.

Craver, C. (2007) *Explaining the brain*, Oxford: Oxford University Press.

Cummins, R. (1975) Functional analysis. *Journal of Philosophy* 72: 741–65.

Cuthbert, B. N. (2014) The RDoC framework: Facilitating transition from ICD/DSM to dimensional approaches that integrate neuroscience and psychopathology. *World Psychiatry* 13: 28–35.

Davidson, A. (1990) Closing up the corpses. In G. Boulos, ed., *Meaning and method*, Cambridge: Cambridge University Press pp.295–326.

Davidson, D. (1980) *Essays on actions and events*, Oxford: Oxford University Press.

Davies, W., Roache, R., and Savulescu, J., eds. (2020) *Psychiatry reborn: Biopsychosocial psychiatry in modern medicine*, Oxford: Oxford University Press.

Demazeux, S., and Singy, P., eds. (2015) *The DSM-5 in perspective philosophical reflections on the psychiatric babel*, Dordrecht: Springer.

Engel, G. L. (1977) The need for a new medical model: A challenge for biomedicine. *Science*, 196(4286): 129–36.

Faucher, L., and Goyer, S. (2015) RDoC: Thinking outside the DSM box without falling into a reductionist trap. In S. Demazeux and P. Singy, eds., *The DSM-5 in perspective*, Dordrecht: Springer Netherlands, pp. 199–224.

Fischer, B. A. (2012) A review of American psychiatry through its diagnoses: The history and development of the diagnostic and statistical manual of mental disorders. *The Journal of Nervous and Mental Disease* 200: 1022–30.

Forest, D., and Faucher, L., eds. (2021) *Defining mental disorders: Jerome Wakefield and his critics*, Cambridge, MA: MIT Press.

Foucault, M. (1989) *Madness and civilisation*, London: Routledge.

Fulford, K. W. M. (1989) *Moral theory and medical practice*, Cambridge: Cambridge University Press.

Fulford, K. W. M. (1999) Nine variations and a coda on the theme of an evolutionary definition of dysfunction. *Journal of Abnormal Psychology* 108: 412–20.

Gould, S. J., and Lewontin, R. C. (1979) The spandrels of San Marco and the Panglossian paradigm: A critique of the adaptationist programme. *Proceedings of the Royal Society, London* 205: 581–98.

Graham, G. (2010) *The disordered mind: An introduction to philosophy of mind and mental illness*, Abingdon: Routledge.

Graham, G. (2013) Ordering disorder: Mental disorder, brain disorder, and therapeutic intervention. In K. W. M. Fulford, M. Davies, R. G. T. Gipps *et al.*, eds., *The Oxford handbook of philosophy and psychiatry*, Oxford: Oxford University Press, pp. 512–30.

Guarnaccia, P. J., and Rogler, L. H. (1999) Research on culture-bound syndromes: New directions. *American Journal of Psychiatry* 156: 1322–7.

Hacking, I. (1991) Making up people. In M. Biagioli, ed., *Science studies reader*, New York: Routledge, pp. 161–71.

Hacking, I. (1999) *The social construction of what?* Cambridge, MA: Harvard University Press.

Haldipur, C., Knoll IV, J., and vd Luft, E., eds. (2019) *Thomas Szasz: An appraisal of his legacy*, Oxford: Oxford University Press.

Hare, R. M. (1952) *The language of morals*, Oxford: Oxford University Press.

Hinton, D. E., Pich, V., Marques, L., Nickerson, A., and Pollack, M. H. (2010) Khyâl attacks: A key idiom of distress among traumatized Cambodia refugees. *Culture, Medicine, and Psychiatry* 34: 244–78.

Horwitz, A. V., and Wakefield, J. C. (2007) *The loss of sadness*, Oxford: Oxford University Press.

Insel, T. R. (2013) Directors blog: Transforming diagnosis. *NIMH*. www .nimh.nih.gov/about/director/2013/transforming-diagnosis.shtml.

Insel, T. R., Cuthbert, B., Garvey, M. *et al.* (2010) Research domain criteria (RDoC): Toward a new classification framework for research on mental disorders. *American Journal of Psychiatry* 167(7): 748–51.

Kelly, B. D., Bracken, P., Cavendish, H. *et al.* (2010) *The Myth of Mental Illness* fifty years after publication: What does it mean today? *Irish Journal of Psychological Medicine* 27: 35–43.

Kendell, R. E. (1975) The concept of disease and its implications for psychiatry. *British Journal of Psychiatry* 127: 305–15.

Kendler, K., and Parnas, J., eds. (2017) *Philosophical issues in psychiatry IV: Classification of psychiatric illness*, Oxford: Oxford University Press.

Kendler, K. S., Zachar, P., and Craver, C. (2011) What kinds of things are psychiatric disorders? *Psychological Medicine* 41: 1143–50.

Kenny, A. J. P. (1969) Mental health in Platos Republic. *Proceedings of the Aristotelian Society*: 55:229–41.

Khalidi, M. (2010) Interactive kinds. *The British Journal for the Philosophy of Science* 61: 335–60.

Khalidi, M. A. (2013) *Natural categories and human kinds: Classification in the natural and social sciences*, Cambridge: Cambridge University Press.

Kim, J. (1993) *Supervenience and mind*, Cambridge: Cambridge University Press.

Kingma, E. (2007) What is it to be healthy? *Analysis* 67: 128–33.

Kingma, E. (2013) Naturalist accounts of mental disorder. In K. W. M. Fulford, M. Davies, R. Gipps., *et al.*, eds., *Oxford handbook of philosophy and psychiatry*, Oxford: Oxford University Press, pp. 363–84.

Kripke, S. (1972) *Naming and necessity*, Cambridge, MA: Harvard University Press.

Kupfer, D. J., First, M. B., and Regier, D. A., eds. (2002) *A research agenda for DSM–V*, Washington, DC: American Psychiatric Association.

Latour, B. (2005) *Reassembling the social: An introduction to actor-network-theory*, Oxford: Oxford University Press.

Lilienfeld, S. O., and Marino, L. (1995) Mental disorder as a Roschian concept: A critique of Wakefields 'harmful dysfunction' analysis. *Journal of Abnormal Psychology* 104: 411–20.

Littlewood, R. (1985) The migration of culture-bound syndromes. In E. Pichot, ed., *Psychiatry the state of the art: Volume 8 history of psychiatry, national schools, education, and transcultural psychiatry*, London: Springer, pp. 703–7.

Littlewood, R. (1986) Russian dolls and Chinese boxes: An anthropological approach to the implicit models of comparative psychiatry. In J. L. Cox, ed., *Transcultural psychiatry*, Beckenham: Croom Helm, pp. 37–58.

Littlewood, R. (2002) *Pathologies of the west*, London: Continuum.

Littlewood, R., and Lipsedge, M. (1986) The culture-bound syndromes of the dominant culture: Culture, psychopathology and biomedicine. In J. L. Cox, ed., *Transcultural psychiatry*, Beckenham: Croom Helm, pp. 253–73.

Mackie, J. L. (1977) *Ethics: Inventing right and wrong*, Harmondsworth: Penguin.

McDowell, J. (1994). *Mind and World*. Harvard: Harvard University Press.

Megone, C. (2000) Mental illness, human function, and values. *Philosophy, Psychiatry and Psychology* 7: 45–65.

Mezzich, J. E., Caracci, G., Fabrega Jr., H., and Kirmayer, L. J. (2009) Cultural formulation guidelines. *Transcultural Psychiatry* 46: 383–405.

Millikan, R. G. (1984) *Language, thought and other biological categories*, Cambridge, MA: MIT Press.

Murphy, D. (2006) *Psychiatry in the scientific image*, Cambridge, MA: MIT Press.

Murphy, D. (2008) Levels of explanation in psychiatry. In K. Kendler and J. Parnas, eds., *Philosophical issues in psychiatry*, Baltimore, MD: The Johns Hopkins University Press, pp. 99–124.

Murphy, D. (2014) Natural kinds in folk psychology and in psychiatry. In H. Kincaid and J. A. Sullivan, eds., *Classifying psychopathology: Mental kinds and natural kinds*, Cambridge, MA: MIT Press, pp. 105–22.

Murphy, D., and Woolfolk, R. L. (2000) The harmful dysfunction analysis of mental disorder. *Philosophy, Psychiatry, and Psychology* 7: 241–52.

Oppenheim, P., and Putnam, H. (1991) Unity of science as a working hypothesis. In R. Boyd, P. Gasper, and J. D. Trout, eds., *Philosophy of science*, London: MIT Press, pp. 405–27.

Parnas, J. (2014) The RDoC program: Psychiatry without psyche? *World Psychiatry* 13: 46–7.

Pickering, N. (2006) *The metaphor of mental illness*, Oxford: Oxford University Press.

Poland, J. (2014) Deeply rooted sources of error and bias in psychiatric classification. In H. Kincaid and J. A. Sullivan, eds., *Classifying psychopathology: Mental kinds and natural kinds*, Cambridge, MA: MIT Press, pp. 29–63.

Putnam, H. (1975) The meaning of meaning. Minnesota Studies in the Philosophy of Science 7: 131–193.

Quinton, A. (1985) Madness. In A. P. Griffiths, ed., *Philosophy and practice*, Cambridge: Cambridge University Press, pp. 17–41.

Radden, J. (2009) *Moody minds distempered: Essays on melancholy and depression*, Oxford: Oxford University Press.

Ryle, G. (1949) *The concept of mind*, London: Hutchinson.

Scull, A. (1989) *Social order/mental disorder: Anglo-American psychiatry in historical perspective*, Berkeley, CA: University of California Press.

Shorter, E. (1997) *A history of psychiatry: From the era of the asylum to the age of Prozac*, New York: John Wiley.

Sober, E. (1984) *The nature of selection*, Cambridge, MA: MIT Press.

Szasz, T. (1960) The myth of mental illness. *American Psychologist* 15: 113–18.

Szasz, T. (1972) *The myth of mental illness*, London: Paladin.

Szasz, T. (1973) Mental illness as metaphor. *Nature* 242: 305–7.

Szasz, T. (1987) *Insanity: the Idea and its Consequences*, New York, John Wiley an Sons.

Szasz, T. (2009) *Antipsychiatry: Quackery squared*, New York: Syracuse University Press.

Tabb, K. (2015) Psychiatric progress and the assumption of diagnostic discrimination. *Philosophy of Science* 82: 1047–58.

Tekin, S., and Bluhm, R., eds. (2019) *The Bloomsbury companion to philosophy of psychiatry*, London: Bloomsbury.

Thornton, T. (2002) Reliability and validity in psychiatric classification: Values and neo-humeanism. *Philosophy Psychiatry and Psychology* 9: 229–35.

Thornton, T. (2007) *Essential philosophy of psychiatry*, Oxford: Oxford University Press.

Thornton, T. (2015) Against explanatory minimalism in psychiatry. *Frontiers of Psychiatry* 6: 171. http://doi.org/10.3389/fpsyt.2015.00171.

Thornton, T. (2019) *John McDowell* (2nd ed.), Abingdon: Routledge.

Thornton, T. (2020) Psychiatry's inchoate wish for a paradigm shift and the bio-psych-social model of mental illness. In W. Davies, R. Roache, and J. Savulescu, eds., *Rethinking biopsychosocial psychiatry*, Oxford: Oxford University Press, pp.229–39.

Tsou, J. (2021) *Philosophy of psychiatry (Elements in the philosophy of science)*, Cambridge: Cambridge University Press.

Wakefield, J. C. (1992) Disorder as harmful dysfunction: A conceptual critique of *DSM-III-R*s definition of mental disorder. *Psychological Review* 99: 232–47.

Wakefield, J. C. (1997a) Diagnosing DSM-IV, part 1: DSM-IV and the concept of mental disorder. *Behavior Research and Therapy* 35: 633–49.

Wakefield, J. C. (1997b) Normal inability versus pathological inability: Why Ossorios definition of mental disorder is not sufficient. *Clinical Psychology: Science and Practice* 4: 249–58.

Wakefield, J. C. (1999) Mental disorder as a black box essentialist concept. *Journal of Abnormal Psychology* 108: 465–72.

Wakefield, J. (200) Aristotle as sociobiologist: The "function of a human being argument, black box essentialism, and the concept of mental disorder. *Philosophy Psychiatry and Psychology* 7:17–44.

Wakefield, J. C. (2014) Wittgensteins nightmare: Why the RDoC grid needs a conceptual dimension. *World Psychiatry* 13(1): 38–40.

White, R., Read, U., Jain, S., and Orr, D., eds. (2017) *The Palgrave handbook of global mental health: Sociocultural perspectives*, London: Palgrave.

Winch, P. ([1958] 1990) *The idea of a social science and its relation to philosophy*, London: Routledge.

Wittgenstein, L. (2009) *Philosophical investigations*, Oxford: Blackwell.

World Health Organization (1992) *The ICD- 10 classification of mental and behavioural disorders: Clinical descriptions and diagnostic guidelines*, Geneva: World Health Organization.

Wright, L. (1973) Functions. *Philosophical Review* 82: 139–68.

Zachar, P., and K.S. Kendler. 2007. Psychiatric disorders: A conceptual taxonomy. American Journal of Psychiatry 164:557–65.

Cambridge Elements ≡

Philosophy of Mind

Keith Frankish

The University of Sheffield

Keith Frankish is a philosopher specializing in philosophy of mind, philosophy of psychology, and philosophy of cognitive science. He is the author of *Mind and Supermind* (Cambridge University Press, 2004) and *Consciousness* (2005), and has also edited or coedited several collections of essays, including *The Cambridge Handbook of Cognitive Science* (Cambridge University Press, 2012), *The Cambridge Handbook of Artificial Intelligence* (Cambridge University Press, 2014) (both with William Ramsey), and *Illusionism as a Theory of Consciousness* (2017).

About the Series

This series provides concise, authoritative introductions to contemporary work in philosophy of mind, written by leading researchers and including both established and emerging topics. It provides an entry point to the primary literature and will be the standard resource for researchers, students, and anyone wanting a firm grounding in this fascinating field.

Cambridge Elements ☰

Philosophy of Mind

Elements in the Series

Mindreading and Social Cognition
Jane Suilin Lavelle

Free Will
Derk Pereboom

Philosophy of Neuroscience
William Bechtel and Linus Ta-Lun Huang

The Metaphysics of Mind
Janet Levin

Mental Illness
Tim Thornton

A full series listing is available at: www.cambridge.org/EPMI

Printed in the United States
by Baker & Taylor Publisher Services